The Blessing of the Prison

Joy Haney

Unless otherwise noted, scripture quotations are from the King James Version of the Holy Bible. Capitalization, italicization, and bold type are for author's emphasis only.

All poetry not credited to another author is written by Joy Haney.

The Blessing of the Prison by Joy Haney
© 1995, Radiant Life Publications

All rights reserved. No portion of this publication may be reproduced, stored in an electronic system, or transmitted, in any form or by any means, electronic, mechanical, photocopying, recording, or otherwise without the prior written permission of the author.

Printed in the United States of America.

ISBN 1-880969-18-1

Table of Contents

	Prologue	5
1.	The Way Up is Down	9
2.	What's Good About a Prison?	21
3.	Prison of Emotional Pain and Rejection	35
4.	Prison of False Accusations	49
5.	Prison of Suffering	61
6.	Prison of Trouble	73
7.	Attitude Makes the Difference	91
8.	Prayer in the Prison	105
9.	Light in the Prison	113
10.	Praise in the Prison	121
11.	Prosper in the Prison	129
12.	Wait Patiently in the Prison	137
13.	The Best is Yet to Come	145
	Notes	151

PROLOGUE

Sitting in a Sunday morning church service in late July 1994, I was given the inspiration by the Lord for a message entitled, *The Blessing of the Prison*. In the margin of my Bible by the story of Joseph in Genesis 39, I wrote these words: *"Blessed, prospered, but still went to prison. Trials prepare for greater things. He was going higher than Potiphar's house."* As I began to study and prepare for this, it seemed as if the Lord would have me put it into book form.

This year has been a year of trials for me, my family, and many of our friends. I feel like there is blood on many of the pages because some of this was written from a bleeding heart. Someone said years ago, "You have to bleed to bless." In those younger days, the idea seemed rather heroic and grandiose. Now after living many years and after having my heart bleed because of the severe trials life has brought, I understand that pain, heartaches, and discipline in the difficult times can produce the greatest things.

THE BLESSING OF THE PRISON

If *you* are encased in the prison of false accusations, suffering, emotional pain, rejection or trouble, remember that Joseph went through the same things, but he had to go down before he went up. His dream could only be fulfilled through his misfortune and sufferings. He went down, but he came up and finally reached his dream because he kept his integrity with God.

> "Amid my list of blessings infinite, stands this the foremost, That my heart has bled."
>
> —Edward Young

THE BLESSING OF THE PRISON

1

THE WAY UP IS DOWN

In London there are 637 steps that lead into the beautiful dome of St. Paul's Cathedral. About nine-tenths of the way up, just at the base of the dome, there is an exit that brings one outside onto a promenade with a marvelous view of the city. If a person is to climb to the apex of the dome, he has to go back inside through a small door on which there is a sign that reads, "Go down, to go up."

Just as one must go down to go up in order to see the dome, many times this same element of truth is essential in reaching a goal or for a dream to be realized. This was true in the life of a handsome young lad named Joseph.

When Joseph was young, the Lord gave him a dream, and from that dream the plan for Joseph's life began to unfold. He was the favored son of Jacob, his father, and was given a special coat of many colors to signify this. One day he was wandering

THE BLESSING OF THE PRISON

through the mountains trying to find his brothers when a man found him and asked him where he was going. He told him that he was trying to find his brothers who were with their flocks. The man told him to go to Dothan and he would find them there. As Joseph neared their camp, he was entering into the first part of the long road towards the fulfillment of his dream. "And when they saw him afar off, even before he came near unto them, they conspired against him to slay him. And they said one to another, Behold, this dreamer cometh" (Genesis 37:18-19).

The circumstances following his misfortunate appearance made it appear that God had forgotten Joseph and his dream. First of all, instead of his brothers welcoming him, they threw him into a pit to be killed by some wild beast. Then because of Judah's reasoning, they roughly hauled Joseph out of the pit and sold him to a band of traveling Ishmeelites, who in turn sold him as a slave to a man named Potiphar, an officer of Pharaoh.

The heart of Joseph was filled with pain from the hate he had received from his brothers, he was among people who did not serve his God, and neither was he a free agent to do as he pleased, however, **while everything appeared to be negative he was still in God's plan.** Genesis 39:2-5 says,

> And the Lord was with Joseph, and he was a prosperous man; and he was in the house of his master the Egyptian. And his master saw that the Lord was with him, and that the Lord made all that he did to prosper in his hand. And Joseph found grace in his sight, and he served him: and he made him overseer over his house, and all that he had he put into his hand. And it came to pass from the time that he had made him overseer in his house, and over all that he had,

that the Lord blessed the Egyptian's house for Joseph's sake; and the blessing of the Lord was upon all that he had in the house, and in the field.

There is a phrase in verse 6 that describes Joseph well. It says, "And Joseph was a goodly person, and well favored."

Even though Joseph had come through temptations number one and two without losing his grip on things, there were more things for him to be tempted with before his dream would come to pass. The Scripture says that Potiphar's wife cast her eyes upon Joseph and tried to seduce him to lie with her. Joseph's integrity with God would not let him do this sinful thing. **You would think that because he did the right thing that everything would turn out alright, but it did not.**

First of all, Potiphar's wife was persistent in her flirtations with Joseph and day after day tried to get him to sin with her. He always said no, but the day came when he went into the house and there was no one inside but her.

> And she caught him by his garment saying, Lie with me; and he left his garment in her hand, and fled, and got him out. And it came to pass, when she saw that he had left his garment in her hand, and was fled forth, That she called unto the men of her house, and spake unto them, saying, See, he hath brought in an Hebrew unto us to mock us; he came in unto me to lie with me, and I cried with a loud voice; and it came to pass, when he heard that I lifted up my voice and cried, that he left his garment with me, and fled, and got him out (Genesis 39:12-15).

THE BLESSING OF THE PRISON

When Potiphar arrived home that evening, she had her strategy well-planned. She lied about Joseph, said that he had tried to seduce her, and then produced his garment that she had grabbed. Potiphar's anger was kindled against Joseph and immediately he had him thrown into the prison. Joseph went, it looked like, the pessimistic way, from the pit to Potiphar's house down into the prison.

It does not matter where you land or what you have to walk through; if you want God to be with you even as He was with Joseph, you must keep your integrity with God. "But the Lord was with Joseph, and shewed him mercy, and gave him favor in the sight of the keeper of the prison" (Genesis 39:21). Not only was He with Joseph, but He made all that he did to prosper (verse 23).

Joseph's dream took him down before it took him up. *It was the prison experience that gave him his final break.* If he had not gone down to the prison, he would have never gone up to the king's palace. God had greater things planned for Joseph than just to be a leader over a household. He wanted him to be a leader over a nation. The main thing to remember is that *Joseph went down, but he came up!* Many times God allows people to experience failure before arriving at their dream.

It was a beautiful day when Joseph stood before Pharaoh the king, and he heard the words that would bring his dream to pass. Pharaoh said,

> Thou shalt be over my house, and according unto thy word shall all my people be ruled: only in the throne will I be greater than thou. And Pharaoh said unto Joseph, See I have set thee over all the land of Egypt. And Pharaoh took off his ring from his hand, and put it upon Joseph's hand,

The Way Up is Down

and arrayed him in vestures of fine linen, and put a gold chain about his neck; And he made him to ride in the second chariot which he had; and they cried before him, Bow the knee: and he made him ruler over all the land of Egypt (Genesis 42:40-43).

All the people could see were the outward trappings of his leadership: the ring, the fine linen, the chariot, the gold, and the pomp and glory. They could not see the pathway that led him there: the false accusations, rejection, pain, loneliness, cold, damp prisons, misunderstandings, the hatred, the fury, the blood, the bleeding heart, and angry lies that marked the pathway to the throne. The glory is always accompanied by suffering and pain. Paul wrote about this concept to younger Timothy. He said, "If we suffer, we shall also reign with him" (II Timothy 2:12).

Some people have the mistaken notion that if a person is living right, that all should go well for him. They look at Psalm 1:3 which describes the blessing of the person who delights in God, and think all will be well. "And he shall be like a tree planted by the rivers of water, that bringeth forth his fruit in his season; his leaf also shall not wither, and whatsoever he doeth shall prosper." **It is true that whatever he does will prosper, but it is also true that he will be tried in the fire.** Joseph's path was mapped out by God to bring about a great work, and even though he was in excruciating circumstances he still prospered wherever he was placed. All the situations that he was thrust into were because of someone else's scheming. Joseph did not choose his pathway. It was chosen by others! But God allowed it for a higher purpose. He had more planned for

THE BLESSING OF THE PRISON

Joseph than just to be the favorite son of his father and to watch the flock on a hillside.

Joseph was chosen by God to do a great work, but the pathway that led him there was strewn with heartache and trials. It is important for you to understand that many times when you are blessed in the Spirit realm, there are those who will be envious of you as others were of Joseph. It is possible that your enemies and even friends will instigate and scheme against you and cause you to experience times of imprisonment, but as it was only temporary for Joseph, so it will be for you. Even though God allowed him to go to prison, he still prospered in the prison. It does not matter where you are placed; if you have a pure heart after God, you will prosper!

This not only happened to Joseph, but also to Daniel. His story is like Joseph's in the fact that he was yanked ruthlessly from a secure family unit into a foreign, heathen country. He, too, prospered even in this new environment to the point where his contemporaries become jealous of him and tried to destroy him. Daniel 6:3 says, "Then this Daniel was preferred above the presidents and princes, because an excellent spirit was in him; and the king thought to set him over the whole realm."

The king's preference brought about Daniel's downfall in the kingdom. He went from top president to the den of lions overnight. Even though Daniel was cast down by the other presidents, God was still with him, and sent an angel to protect him. If Daniel had not have gone down into the den of lions, he would have stayed on the same level. God had greater plans for him. He had to go down before going up. After he had been brought up out of the den and the jealous men had been thrown to the lions, the king then made a decree that all the people of the land would serve Daniel's God. Daniel 6:28 says, "So this

The Way Up is Down

Daniel prospered in the reign of Darius, and in the reign of Cyrus the Persian."

The same is true of the Apostle Paul. He was in prison often, but because he was forced to be still in one place, much of the New Testament was written there. Chafing because he could not go and preach to the churches, he wrote letters which have immortalized his name and have been carrying God's message to all generations since. His prison experiences were necessary for God's greater plan of saving many people.

The three discussed in this chapter, Joseph, Daniel, and Paul, were alike in four ways:

1. They were God-conscious.
2. They were men of prayer.
3. They had dreams and visions and did not scoff at spiritual experiences. They were a part of their life and each of the men was motivated by them.
4. They had thankful spirits.

If you walk with the Lord long enough, you will find sometime in your life a kinship with these three men who found themselves to be prisoners because of their dreams and integrity with God.

Not only does this happen to those who walk with God, but also to those who share a dream to help mankind. There are thousands of cases, even in the natural, that prove that one often has to suffer failure, heartbreak, or pain before he enjoys success or blessing. What seems like a failure is often a blessing, if a person has integrity.

This happened to Stephen Girard. When he was 26 years old, he made a sea record as the successful captain of a

THE BLESSING OF THE PRISON

merchant vessel sailing from French ports to the West Indies. But in May 1776, disaster came. A storm and fog drove him to take his ship into Delaware Bay. The British fleet was hovering near, and it was unwise for him to attempt to escape. He landed at Philadelphia, and soon was a captain without a ship, a seaman who could not leave the land, a man far from the country with whose ways he was acquainted.

Surely this was failure. But Stephen Girard was not ready to fail. Within two years he was an American citizen and within fifteen years he was the leading Philadelphia ship owner. His ships sailed to all parts of the world. Thirty-six years after he was compelled to change his life plans, he became his country's banker during the War of 1812. When public credit after the war was at so low an ebb that only $20,000 was subscribed to the $5,000,000 loan offered, he stepped into the breach and subscribed for the rest. The act restored confidence and the people clamored for the bonds.

This is true also in the case of Henry Bessenger. What seemed like a failure was really a blessing. When he was a young man he perfected a plan for the use of revenue stamps that promised to save the British government large sums. As a recognition he was promised a comfortable position in the employ of the government. But just when he was ready to grasp his reward a fatal flaw was revealed in his stamp plan. The easy position slipped from his grasp.

He had failed. Fortunately he did not lose courage, though he realized that a life of struggle was before him. The struggle bore rich fruit, however, for within a few years he became the inventor of the process of steel making which made his name famous and proved of incalculable benefit to the world. But what if, succeeding in the first invention, he had landed in the government booth?

If you are living right, following God's Word the best you know how, and are subjected to trials such as Joseph experienced, look up today, for God has greater things for you. He sees you doing well over the things He has placed in your care, and is going to place more leadership or responsibility into your hands. So continue to walk with a pure heart after God no matter what you are going through, and God's plan will emerge even out of the heartache and pain.

God prepares people through the school of hardship. Moses could not be polished in the king's palace. He was prepared on the back side of a desert *after* tragedy struck his life. David, the successor to the throne after Saul, could not be sufficiently prepared singing songs for the king in the palace. He became a fugitive hiding in dens and caves *after* King Saul tried to kill him. The loneliness, ruggedness, and privations helped to shape David for the kingship.

It is often the hurtful things that cause the knee to bow low, that usher in the greatest preparation for the work God has prepared for you.

THE BLESSING OF THE PRISON

"I thank God for my handicaps, for through them, I have found myself, my work, and my God."

—Helen Keller

THE BLESSING OF THE PRISON

2

WHAT'S GOOD ABOUT A PRISON?

A prison cell is narrow, it boxes one in.
It shuts out the light, makes all dark within.
Access to other worlds is barred and shut.
Freedom is a memory, life becomes a rut.

Doors close with jarring, clanging sounds.
The prisoner is stifled by the guard's continual rounds.
Though his body is enclosed inside a small cell,
He feels like he has slipped into an abyss of hell.

He wonders if he will ever again see the dawn,
Now that life's luxury and excesses are gone.
The startling fact of what matters most,
Must now be reckoned with, not previous loud boasts.

THE BLESSING OF THE PRISON

It is the attitude and condition of the mind,
That causes the prisoner to see, or strikes him blind.
He alone imprisons himself, feeling alone and forlorn,
Or he can soar with the eagles in the sky, feeling reborn.

Though stripped, and locked up, and barely a copin'
The world of the mind can still be left open.
So force yourself to think, pray, and be still,
And cease from anger and exercise the human will!

All emotional prisons are not forever!
Do not be guilty of saying, "I'll never, I'll never!"
This can be the best time of your life—even now.
So purpose in your heart to rise above the hurt somehow.

Put the past behind you, forgive and forget.
Do not stay under the load of an emotional debt!
Rise up and stretch, reach for the stars.
As you leave behind you those prison bars!

The hurtful things of life will make you better.
They will help to loose the chains of life's dark fetters.
For when you are hurting, Jesus stands very near,
To give you strength and faith, and take away your fear.

Let your prison experience teach you how to bless the throngs.
Let your tears become pearls and your pain become songs!
Become the unmarred vessel in the darkness of your night.
And may you shine with Christ's love and His brilliant light!

What's Good About a Prison?

Jeremiah portrays a vivid picture of the potter's house. He explains when the potter looks at a vessel and finds flaws, he either throws it in the potter's field or he puts it back on the potter's wheel to make it more perfect and unmarred. "And the vessel that he made of clay was marred in the hand of the potter: so he made it again another vessel, as seemed good to the potter to make it" (Jeremiah 18:4).

Literal prisons used for criminals are to help reform or change them, to make them better citizens or better people. Spiritual prisons, likewise, are to help bring the good out in a person. They are so that a *diamond in the rough* can be spiritually polished to greater value and glory.

Every Christian needs to come to a place where God is truly Lord of his life. He is the potter that is in charge of all things. He makes the vessel, the vessel does not make itself. Bill Vaughn said, "Stormy weather is what man needs from time to time to remind him he's not really in charge of anything." [1] In other words, man is not sufficient in himself; he needs God. Not only does he need God, but he needs to let God be God and let Him be the total Leader or Director of his life.

Prison experiences are good for people *only* if they allow themselves to learn, excel or grow from them. They can enrich a life as nothing else can. Madame Swetchine said, "Those who have suffered much are like those who know many languages; they have learned to understand all and be understood by all." [2]

Prisons are places of confinement, causing one to cease from regular activities. They help free the mind to think on the possibilities of the future. Prison provides a time for re-evaluation and a time to get priorities right. Wise King Solomon wrote, "Sorrow is better than laughter: for by the sadness of the countenance the heart is made better" (Ecclesiastes 7:3).

THE BLESSING OF THE PRISON

> Tis sorrow builds the shining ladder up,
> Whose golden rounds are our calamities,
> Whereon our firm feet planting, nearer God
> The spirit climbs, and hath its eyes unsealed.
>
> *James Russel Lowell* [3]

No one in his right mind would willingly ask for sorrow or shut himself up in a prison, but if life hands you a prison experience, it can be the thing that takes you from mediocrity to excellence, if you allow it to happen. *Good things can happen in a prison that would probably not have happened otherwise.*

Sir Walter Scott once said, "Give me my imagination and I can be happy in a prison." Sir Walter Raleigh, upon the death of Queen Elizabeth, came into disfavor in court and was imprisoned in the Tower of London for thirteen years. But they could not shut up or chain his active mind and spirit. He wrote a remarkable history of the world which was considered a classic in the century that followed.

John Bunyan was shut up in a Bedford jail that he might not preach the gospel. Because his soul refused to be enchained, he wrote what was for centuries the most popular book written in the English language, *Pilgrim's Progress*.

The Apostle John, who was banished to the Isle of Patmos and left to die, received revelations from God and wrote what is the most blessed book of the Bible: The Revelation. Martin Luther, who was thrown into a prison at Wartburg Castle for his religious beliefs, translated the Bible into the German language. Madam Buyon's sweetest poems and deepest experiences were from long imprisonments.

What's Good About a Prison?

Cervantes, who wrote hundreds of novels, stories and poems, joined up as a mercenary in a European army, and when they were beaten, he was among those who were imprisoned. So he began a novel. He finished one chapter and read it to his fellow prisoners and they liked it. He kept writing and reading it to his captive audience until he finished the book, *Don Quixote*. He was in his fifties when he wrote this famous book.

An anonymous author wrote, "God seems to exact as His price of 'best-selling' writing success a diploma from His grueling School of Experience. Courses are: Discipline, Suffering, Faith, Tests, and Self-examination." [4]

"When the Confederate army retreated after Gettysburg, General Lee wrote to Jefferson Davis a remarkable letter, saying: 'We must expect reverses, even defeats. They are sent to teach us wisdom and prudence, to call forth greater energies, and to prevent our falling into greater disasters.'" [5]

Prison experiences can draw a person closer to the Lord. Grace Robinson shares a prayer by an Ethiopian at Soddu, Ethiopia. He prayed,

> Almighty God, from the depth of my heart I plead with thee to send us trouble. When our king was exiled we were in much trouble with the foreign rulers. We had to meet in secret and were in constant danger of our lives. That was the time when we worked in harmony with our fellow Christians.
>
> Many a night after I had locked my door and gone to bed, tired from a day's long journey of preaching and teaching, there came a persistent knocking. Lord, how I wanted to sleep, and surely they wouldn't want to be baptized at night and be hunted and chased and put in prison

THE BLESSING OF THE PRISON

and beaten, but they said they had seen the Christians' joy and they too wanted that religion. Every night there were more and more.
We read Thy Word and talked about it and prayed through the nights. We shared our joy in the Lord. We worked side by side with only one desire, to preach and teach the Gospel. Then, Lord, our king came back. The foreign rulers were forced to leave our country.
We have peace in our land. We baptize in the daytime. We are not beaten. We meet and pray, yes, but we are beginning to grow careless in our zeal for Thee. Jealousies creep in and spoil the harmony. Petty troubles take on in large meetings. We are selfish in our ambitions. Dear Lord, send us more trouble, I pray Thee, that we may forget ourselves and be so dependent on Thee that we have no time to become selfish and jealous of our fellow Christians. For Jesus' sake. Amen. [6]

The Lord never willingly hurts anyone. He allows trouble, as the Ethiopian pointed out in his prayer, because many times trouble and pain humble us and draw us closer to God and to each other. A skilled physician was about to perform a delicate operation and said reassuringly to his patient, "I may hurt you, but I will not injure you." The purpose of Christ for His children is for them to have a richer, more abundant life, and that is accomplished through hurtful trials. The deeper the trial, the richer the gold! Job said, "But he knoweth the way that I take: when he hath tried me, I shall come forth as gold" (Job 23:10).

Let thy gold be cast in the furnace,
Thy red gold, precious and bright;

Do not fear the hungry fire,
With its caverns of burning light;

And thy gold shall return more precious,
Free from every spot and stain;
For gold must be tried by fire,
As a heart must be tried by pain.

In the cruel fire of Sorrow
Cast thy heart, do not faint or wail;
Let thy hand be firm and steady
Do not let thy spirit quail:

But wait till the trial is over;
And take thy heart again;
For as gold is tried by fire;
So a heart must be tried by pain!

Adelaide Anne Proctor [7]

Samuel L. Brengle's little classic, *Helps to Holiness*, was originally written as a series of articles. It was penned during a period of convalescence after a tough young boy threw a whole paving brick at the author's head. The Brengles used to say:

If there had been no little brick,
There would have been no little book. [8]

Mrs. Brengle kept the brick and painted a text on it: "But as for you, ye thought evil against me; but God meant it unto

THE BLESSING OF THE PRISON

good, to bring to pass, as it is this day to save much people alive" (Genesis 50:20).

Prison experiences not only draw us closer to the Lord and help us become more fruitful, but they help rid us of self-satisfaction that keeps us on the same level too long.

"A young artist had produced an exquisite picture, the most successful of all his efforts, and even his master found nothing in it to criticize. But the young artist was so enraptured with it that he incessantly gazed at his work of art, and really believed that he would never be able to excel what he had already produced.

"One morning, as he was about to enjoy anew the contemplation of his picture, he found his master had entirely erased his work of art. Angry, and in tears, he ran to his master and asked the cause of this cruel treatment.

"The master answered, 'I did it with wise forethought. The painting was good, but it was at the same time your ruin.' 'How so?' asked the young artist. 'My beloved pupil,' replied the master, 'You love no longer your art in your picture, but only yourself. Believe me, it was not perfect, even if it did appear so; it was only a study attempt. Take your pencil and see what your new creation will be, and do not repent of the sacrifice.'

"The student seized his pencil and produced his masterpiece: *The Sacrifice of Ighigenia*. His name was Timanthes." [9]

When we become too full of self and cease to grow and improve, the Master will allow something to happen that shakes us out of our self-satisfaction. He knows that anyone who ceases to reach and grow, stretch and do, will shrivel and die eventually. Prison experiences many times stretch the soul, expand the mind, and bring out the best in a person. They will either make you strong or brittle, sweet or bitter. An unknown author wrote,

> There was never a picture painted,
> There was never a poem sung,
> But the soul of the artist fainted,
> And the poet's heart was wrung.

Great things are often times born out of sorrow and trouble. Author Ruth Sanderson shows how God prepared Abraham Lincoln to be President over a divided country this way. She writes:

"Seeking a deliverer and a saviour, the great God in His own purpose passed by the palace, and its silken delights.

"He took a little babe in His arms and called to His side His favorite angel, the angel of sorrow.

"Stooping He whispered, 'O Sorrow, thou well beloved teacher, take thou this child of mine and make him great.

"'Take him to yonder cabin in the wilderness; make his home a poor man's home; plant his narrow path thick with thorns; cut his little feet with sharp rocks as he climbs the hill of difficulty.

"'Make each footprint red with his own life blood; load his little back with burdens; give to him days of toil and nights of study and sleeplessness.

"'Wrest from his arms whatever he loves; make his heart, through sorrow, as sensitive to the sigh of a slave as a thread of silk in a window is sensitive to the slightest wind that blows; and when you have digged lines of pain in his cheek and make

his face more marred than the face of any man of his time, bring him back to me, and with him I will free 4,000,000 slaves.'
"That is how God made Abraham Lincoln." [10]

It is not the easy things that train a person, it is the difficult moments that can put steel and iron inside them. Beecher wrote about a truth she learned from a bed of asters. She wrote, "I had a bed of asters last summer, that reached clear across my garden in the country. Oh, how gaily they bloomed. They were planted late. On the sides were yet fresh blossoming flowers, while the tops had gone to seed. Early frosts came, and I found one day that long line of radiant beauty was seared, and I said, 'Ah! the season is too much for them; they have perished'; and I bade them farewell.

"I disliked to go and look at the bed, it looked so like a graveyard of flowers. But, four or five weeks ago one of my men called my attention to the fact that along the whole line of that bed there were asters coming up in the greatest abundance; and I looked, and behold, for every plant that I thought the winter had destroyed there were fifty plants that it had planted. What did those frosts and surly winds do?

"They caught my flowers, they slew them, they cast them to the ground, they trod with snowy feet upon them, and they said, leaving their work, 'This is the end of you.' And the next spring there were for every root, fifty witnesses to rise up and say, 'By death we live.'

"And as it is in the floral tribe, so it is in God's Kingdom. By death came everlasting life. By crucifixion and the sepulcher came the throne and the palace of the Eternal God. By overthrow came victory. Do not be afraid to suffer. Do not be afraid to be overthrown.

What's Good About a Prison?

"It is by being cast down and not destroyed; it is by being shaken to pieces, and the pieces torn to shreds, that men become men of might, and that one a host; whereas men that yield to the appearance of things, and go with the world, have their quick blossoming, their momentary prosperity and then their end, which is an end forever." [11]

What is good about a prison? It draws people down into a narrow place and makes them aware of things they tend to ignore when they were busy with so many other things. A prison experience gives you **time for**:

P planning; to evaluate priorities. It is a forced *pause* in life.

R reflection; renewal

I improvement; in-depth thinking

S settling, strengthening, and productive solitude

O opportunity to review objectives and observe direction.

N negotiating: coming to terms with life; surmounting obstacles.

A prison experience can also be likened to times of trial. Peter gives the reason for these times in I Peter 5:10. "But the God of all grace, who hath called us unto his eternal glory by Christ Jesus, after that ye have **suffered** awhile, make you *perfect, stablish, strengthen, settle* you."

THE BLESSING OF THE PRISON

Psalm 105:17-19 says the Lord tried Joseph. "He sent a man before them, even Joseph, who was sold for a servant: Whose feet they hurt with fetters: he was laid in iron: Until the time that his word came: the word of the Lord tried him." Joseph needed the prison experience to prepare him for greater things. *He had to go down before he went up.* Author J.H. Evans wrote, "If you ask the way to the crown—'tis by the cross; to the mountain—'tis by the valley; to exaltation—'tis he that humbleth himself." [12]

"As threshing separates the wheat from the chaff, so does affliction purify virtue."

—Richard E. Burton

THE BLESSING OF THE PRISON

3

PRISON OF EMOTIONAL PAIN AND REJECTION

Cold, ruthless, and murderous are words that describe Joseph's brothers. At one time these brothers were young, sweet, and innocent. Something happened to them in their adulthood. They became envious, bitter, and evil. Anyone who would devise the death of someone simply because he was a dreamer is partially insane by anger. Their excuse was that he was a dreamer. They said, when they saw him coming towards them, "Behold, this dreamer cometh." They did not talk about his evil ways, his obnoxious mannerisms, or his bad character. All they could indict him for was that he talked about his dreams too much. This made them jealous to the point that they wanted to shut him up forever.

Until you have been rejected by someone you love, you can never know what Joseph felt. It is a pain so deep that tears at the very soul of a person. It whispers lies, accuses and brings insecurity. The raw loneliness, the salty tears and the broken heart are all that remain for a period of time. There are times when your insides heave with desperation. You cannot form words; the pain is so deep, all you can do is groan.

It was also cold, ruthless, icy, chilly spirits that characterized the callused, insensitive, hardened men who watched a sorrowful Judas humble himself and ask to be released from his bloody bargain. "Then Judas, which had betrayed him [Jesus], when he saw that he was condemned, repented himself, and brought again the thirty pieces of silver to the chief priests and elders, saying, I have sinned in that I have betrayed the innocent blood. And they said, what is that to us?" (Matthew 27:3-4).

"What is that to us?" sneeringly spoken by heartless religious leaders showed they cared more about money than they did a tortured soul. Is there anything more horrendously awful than a we-do-not-care-about-you attitude when someone is in trouble?

This attitude has been characteristic of people down through the ages. Cain killed Abel because he cared more about his own interests than those of his brother. King Saul chased David like a hunted animal because he cared only for his own self. Joseph's brothers would have killed him if Reuben had not intervened. Their attitude was, "Let's get rid of Joseph because he thinks he is better than us." They did not care enough about him to listen and try to understand. They cared more about their own selfish selves. They ruthlessly sold Joseph to strangers and sent him on his way, totally alone.

Sometimes when you are in the prison of emotional pain or rejection, this same insensitive and unfeeling spirit is transferred to you. Others may not say it, but you sense it screaming at

Prison of Emotional Pain and Rejection

you. They infer by their attitude, "What is that to us? It is your problem, you deal with it."

So once more like Joseph you travel the road alone wishing you had someone who really cared and understood—not only understand, but that would empathize with you. You long for a warm, caring heart, for someone to say, "I care, let me help you."

If all you encounter are people with chilly smiles, icy eyes, and hardened hearts, do not give up as Judas did. He went and hanged himself. Even if you feel you have no one, you do have Someone. It is reassuring to have a pair of eyes to look into and a sympathetic ear to hear you when you are talking. It is nice to have someone you can touch, but if you do not have anyone to touch or talk to in the physical realm, you do have Jesus. He is greater than any person could ever be, for He always understands. His mercy endureth forever! It is not on consignment or ration. He will never say, "What is that to me?"

His heart is touched by just the *feeling* of the infirmity. He not only will listen, but He will help rescue you and give you new hope. The greatest thing you need to guard against when you have been rejected is becoming hardened and bitter. It is imperative that you keep the light on in your heart, even when the light goes out around you. Other prisoners may curse, swear and give up hope, but you must seek to keep your eyes upon the invisible Jesus instead of the visible rats.

The word *rejection* has a raw-sounding edge to it. It seethes with stubborn misunderstanding and is riddled with the bullets of icy coldness. The inner man thrust into deep pain cannot cease from crying bitter tears of loneliness and despair. It is one of the loneliest words in the English language. It stands utterly alone! There is no warmth, no caring, no love, and utter dejection settles into the mind of the rejected one.

A minister shared with me how everything seemingly was going alright in his life. He had his dreams and secure plans when suddenly his world was ripped apart by the "brethren." He was a pastor who was falsely accused, and made to feel that he had never done anything for the church that schemed against him. One day he was pastor; the night of the final board meeting he was not!

Going home to his precious wife, they wept together and the raw hurt of rejection crept into the very sinew of their bones and spirit. The questioning of the call began. The questions about their future and effectiveness came like tormenting demons to haunt them. As they prayed, travailed and wept at their own crucifixion, he said, "Lord, I'm finished."

Shortly after that prayer, another pastor from out of state called and asked him to come and preach for him. He accepted, and before the pastor gave him the pulpit he asked how many people in the congregation had been touched or influenced by this visiting preacher. Quite a few hands went up and the pastor had some of the people testify. One after another they told how the visiting preacher had helped or changed their life for the better. About that time, the Lord whispered to him, "I am not finished with you yet. As you have helped these, you will help many more find Me."

Not long after that night the Lord opened a door for him that would cause him to be able to influence many more people for the Lord Jesus than at the location that had been so "secure" for him. As Joseph said it, he could say it. "Ye meant evil unto me, but God meant it unto good."

Prison of Emotional Pain and Rejection

Not only did Joseph suffer emotional pain and rejection, he also suffered the humiliation of being ignored. When Potiphar had him put in prison, he met two of the king's servants who were in there for a short period. While in prison they both had dreams which Joseph interpreted for them. Joseph told the butler, when he was finally restored to his position by the king's side, to remember him to the king, but the butler forgot about Joseph. For two years he was totally ignored by those that knew he had a special gift of interpretation. He could do something no one else could do as well as him, but instead of being used, he was left to rot in a prison, overlooked by those in authority.

Joseph felt the pain of listening about others doing what he wanted to do, but never had opportunity to do, simply because he was never asked. The tears he felt inside became the water that polished the rough edges to his personality. He did not get angry about being ignored, but simply kept doing what he was doing the best he could under the circumstances, until finally he was chosen to do something greater. No longer was he ignored, he was chosen.

If you are living right, to the best of your ability, and something bad happens to you and you seemingly are rejected or ignored by those you respect or love, do not let it destroy you. It is to polish you and prepare you for greater things! Remember, if Joseph had not been rejected by Potiphar and banished to the prison, he might not have ever reached the throne and realized his dreams.

God has His eye upon you just as He did Joseph. He only allows that to happen to you which will make you more like Him, and bring you into greater things. The choice is up to you. When you are rejected you can live in the state of dejection and

THE BLESSING OF THE PRISON

be depressed forever, or you can be delivered from that state by your performance in the prison. Do not feel like you are all alone, for you are not. The Lord is with you even in your pain.

Someone wrote a song that expresses the doubt in the prison. It says:

> Does Jesus care when my heart is pained,
> Too deeply for mirth or song,
> As the burdens press,
> And the cares distress,
> And the way grows weary and long?
>
> Does Jesus care when my way is dark,
> With a nameless dread and fear?
> When for my deep grief
> There is no relief,
> Tho' my tears flow all the night long?

The third stanza answers it by saying:

> O Yes, He cares, I know He cares,
> His heart is touched with my grief;
> When the days are weary,
> The long nights dreary,
> I know my Saviour cares. [1]

If He cares, why does God allow some things to stay in a person's life, when he prays otherwise?

There are times when God allows something to stay in the life of a believer because it is the very thing that will bring him glory, or keep him close to the Lord of the cross. The emotional distress of a situation will keep some people praying, or in a humbled position so the Lord can use them for His glory.

Paul wrote in II Corinthians 4:8-10, "We are troubled on every side, yet not distressed; we are perplexed, but not in despair; Persecuted, but not forsaken; cast down, but not destroyed; Always bearing about in the body the **dying** of the Lord Jesus, that the **life** also of Jesus might be made manifest in our body." He coupled death with life.

In II Corinthians 12 Paul went on to explain how God allowed a *thorn* to stay in his life. He talked about his great visions and revelations, how he was caught up into paradise and heard unspeakable words, but in those things he said he would not glory. He said,

> Of such an one will I glory: yet of myself I will not glory, but in mine infirmities. For though I would desire to glory, I shall not be a fool; for I will say the truth: but now I forbear, lest any man should think of me above that which he seeth me to be, or that he heareth of me. And lest I should be exalted above measure through the abundance of the revelations, there was given to me a thorn in the flesh, the messenger of Satan to buffet me, lest I should be exalted above measure. For this thing I besought the Lord thrice, that it might depart from me. And he said unto me, My grace is sufficient for thee: for my strength is made perfect in weakness. Most gladly therefore will I rather glory in my infirmities, that the power of Christ may rest upon me. Therefore I take pleasure in infirmities, in reproaches, in necessities, in persecutions, in distresses for Christ's sake: for when I am weak, then am I strong (II Corinthians 12:5-10).

THE BLESSING OF THE PRISON

This was the Paul that, when a viper fastened on his hand, he just shook off the beast into the fire, and felt no harm (Acts 28:3-4). This was the Paul who continually performed miracles through the power of God, and from his body were sent forth handkerchiefs or aprons so that diseases and evil spirits departed from the ones that touched them (Acts 19:11-12). This was the same man that prayed such a powerful prayer that the Lord sent an earthquake and the prison doors were opened (Acts 16:25-26).

He could have become exalted, but God kept him aware of His sovereignty and power.

John Wesley had a terrible wife. "She tormented him beyond measure. But he said that he attributed most of his success to his wife—that she kept him on his knees and because he was kept on his knees, he had the victory." [2]

Some people want to use the scripture about the thorn as a cop-out. They do not want to "pray until," fight demonic spirits or press through to victory, so they say, "Well, it must not be the Lord's will to answer my prayer." You pray with faith until! Let God decide what needs to stay in your life, and if He keeps something in your life to keep you on your knees, then let the purpose be accomplished. As the perfume comes from the crushed rose, let it also come from your crushing or breaking. Do not exist in misery and depression, but seek to let the glory of the Lord reign in your life.

Author A.C. Dixon writes,

> Paul did not take pleasure in infirmities. He tells us that he was anxious to get rid of the infirmity that clouded his life. But when he saw that God supplied the grace he began to love the supply better than freedom from infirmity. He saw

that it was better to have darkness with stars brought out by it, than all sunshine and no stars; that the cold winds of winter are as necessary for the world's development as the cheerful warmth of spring and summer; that the mantle of snow is as good for earth as its mantle of grass and flowers. When a man learns that God's strength is perfected through his infirmity, necessities, persecutions, and distresses, he will by and by begin to welcome them as an angel sent from heaven to minister to him. [3]

Sometimes God will let you carry a cross because it is the load of that cross that keeps your knees bowed to the ground in submission to Him. The very thing that causes you to bleed becomes your glory.

George Matheson, a blind Scotch preacher, wrote many years ago these words:

> There is a time coming in which your glory shall consist in the very thing which now constitutes your pain. Nothing could be more sad to Jacob than the ground on which he was lying, a stone for his pillow! It was the hour of his poverty. It was the season of his night. It was the seeming absence of his God. The Lord was in the place and he knew it not. Awakened from his sleep he found that the day of his trial was the dawn of his triumph! Ask the great ones of the past what has been the spot of their prosperity and they will say, "It was the cold ground on which I was lying." Ask Abraham; he will point you to the sacrifice on Mount Moriah. Ask Joseph; he will direct you to his dungeon. Ask Moses; he will date his fortune from his danger in the Nile. Ask Ruth; she will bid you build her monument in the field

of her toil. Ask David; he will tell you that his songs came from the night. Ask Job; he will remind you that God answered him out of the whirlwind. Ask Peter; he will extol his submersion in the sea. Ask John; he will give the path to Patmos. Ask Paul; he will attribute his inspiration to the light which struck him blind. Ask *one more!*—the Son of God. Ask Him whence has come His rule over the world; He will answer, "From the cold ground on which I was lying —the Gethsemane ground—I received my scepter there." Thou too, my soul, shall be garlanded by Gethsemane! The cup thou fain wouldest pass from thee will be thy coronet in the sweet by and by.

The hour of thy loneliness will crown thee. The day of thy depression will regale thee. It is thy desert that will break forth into singing. It is the trees of thy silent forest that will clap their hands. The last things will be first, in the sweet by and by. The thorns will be roses. The vales will be hills. The crooks will be straight lines, the ruts will be level. The shadows will be shining. The losses will be promotions. The tears will be tracks of gold. The voice of God to thine evening will be this: "Thy treasure is hid in the ground, where thou wert lying." [4]

George Matheson also said,

My God, I have never thanked Thee for my *thorn!* I have thanked Thee a thousand times for my roses, but never once for my *thorn*; I have been looking forward to a world where I shall get compensation for my cross as itself a present glory. Teach me the glory of my cross; teach me the value of my *thorn*. Show me that I have climbed to Thee by the path of pain. Show me that my tears have made my rainbow. [5]

THE BLESSING OF THE PRISON

"The gem cannot be polished without friction, nor man perfected without trials."

—Chinese proverb

THE BLESSING OF THE PRISON

4

PRISON OF FALSE ACCUSATIONS

They nailed me to a tree. They crucified me.
Their words were like blows, which shattered my soul!
My heart was broken, I was alone.
The world danced on merrily, while my spirit groaned.

The heaviness of the load, the darkness of the night.
Shoved me deeper in the pit, while those that put me there, spit!
Cleverly they plotted; they worked and they schemed,
Joining in with the demons, or so it seemed.

To accuse, condemn, and strip me with words so cruel and cold.
Their accusations were as daggers designed to make me fall and lose my hold.

THE BLESSING OF THE PRISON

All the while they were crying out boldly their innocence loud and clear,
While I was tempted to huddle in a mass of tears and fear.

Then I remembered Joseph who dreamed so long ago.
Who made his brothers envious, how he was hated so.
The Lord had greater things for Joseph that he could ever dream!
But first he must go down into the pit and prison, a victim of evil schemes.

As I lay seemingly stretched on a man-made cross,
I reflected upon Joseph's excruciating pain and great loss.
Then I thought of the dear Saviour who suffered pain and died,
He suffered and was rejected; about Him they also lied.

He was stripped of dignity, falsely accused, mocked and humiliated.
Made a common criminal, dying between two thieves, His heart bled.
But He had to go down before He went up.
Before the glory, He had to drink the bitter cup.

But He rose up and ascended into heaven with the keys of death and hell in His hands.
Because of Him we can bear the pain of those who would hurt or misunderstand.
And as they meant evil unto Him, God meant it only unto good, to bring a crown.
It's always been and it will always be, before you go up, you must go down!

Prison of False Accusations

Even though this is true, it still hurts to be falsely accused. Psalm 79:11 gives hope to those who are sentenced to die in the prison of false accusation. It says, "Let the sighing of the prisoner come before thee; according to the greatness of thy power preserve thou those that are appointed to die." Many times in this kind of a trial you pray for something to happen, but you finally realize if anything good happens, it will be the Lord's doing. While waiting, you cry, "Bring my soul out of prison" (Psalm 142:7). You groan in your trouble and are comforted by Psalm 102:19-20: "For he hath looked down from the height of his sanctuary; from heaven did the Lord behold the earth; To hear the groaning of the prisoner; to loose those that are appointed to death."

What do you do when you are falsely accused? Abraham Lincoln made the following statement when his enemies accused him falsely:

> If I tried to read, much less answer, all the criticisms made of me, and all the attacks leveled against me, this office would have to be closed for all other business. I do the best I know how, the very best I can. And I mean to keep on doing this, down to the very end. If the end brings me out all wrong, ten angels swearing I had been right would make no difference. If the end brings me out all right, then what is said against me now will not amount to anything. [1]

You can either run around trying to straighten everything out, or you can do what Abraham Lincoln did. He kept on doing what he was doing the best he knew how according to the dictates of his heart. He did not waste his time trying to put

THE BLESSING OF THE PRISON

out brush fires of false accusations, but allowed the fires to burn while doing what he felt to be right.

Colonel George Washington Goethals came up against the same problem. "While contending with the manifold problems of geography and climate in the building of the Panama Canal, Colonel George Washington Goethals had to endure the carping criticism of countless busybodies back home who freely predicted that he would never complete his great task. But the resolute builder pressed steadily forward in his work and said nothing.

"'Aren't you going to answer your critics?' a subordinate inquired.

"'In time,' Goethals replied.

"'How?'

"The great engineer smiled.

"'With the canal,' he replied." [2]

From a 19th century book comes this advice to those who come under attack from criticism:

> Silence is often the best answer to criticism. Sometimes a man's steady, faithful work is his defense. Ole Bull, the violinist, was once offered space in the *New York Herald* to answer his detractors. He said: "I think it is best that they write against me and I play against them." The finest argument against one's detractors is a faithful doing of the very best one can do. It disarms criticism. It wins sympathy. It wastes no time and suffers no loss. Practical doing is ever better than fault finding or trying to satisfy the censorious. And the world knows it. [3]

Prison of False Accusations

Jesus used this method. When He stood before Caiaphas and the Sanhedrin, "...many false witnesses came..." (Matthew 26:60). "But Jesus held his peace" (Matthew 26:63). Then when He stood before Pilate and Pilate said, "...Hearest thou not how many things they witness against thee? And he answered him to never a word; insomuch that the governor marvelled greatly" (Matthew 27:13-14).

Other times Jesus answered them with strong words. When they accused Him of being a winebibber, He addressed the lie (Luke 7:34). When they accused Him of having a devil, Jesus refuted their accusation saying, "I have not a devil" (John 8:49). They became so angry with Jesus that they picked up stones to cast at Him, but Jesus hid Himself. There is a time to speak and a time to retreat. Pray that God will give you the wisdom to know which to do.

Jesus also gave forth words of wisdom on proper conduct toward those that would despitefully use you and toward those that would hate you. Hate usually erupts into some kind of false accusation. It is usually colored to make the one talked about look bad, while the informer is made to look good. Jesus said, "But I say unto you, Love your enemies, bless them that curse you, do good to them that hate you, and pray for them which despitefully use you, and persecute you" (Matthew 5:44). The key words are: **love, bless, pray,** and **do good!**

It is not easy to love someone who has spoken falsely against you. Why bless someone that is wicked? How can you do good to someone that rejects you and treats you like dirt? What kind of doctrine is this? It is impossible to do this! This is the reasoning of the one who is falsely accused, and yes, it is impossible to do this in man's strength.

THE BLESSING OF THE PRISON

This is where the humbling process enters. Man goes down on his knees and begins to weep and pray because of the piercing of the heart. As he begins to pray, something happens. The Lord enters the scene. David wrote, "The Lord is nigh unto them that are of a broken heart; and saveth such as be of a contrite spirit" (Psalm 34:18). When God becomes involved in a situation, then the miracle occurs. Where once there was hate, vengeance, and despair, He changes those feelings to mercy, forgiveness, and hope.

There cannot be love, blessing and the doing of good until first there is prayer. Prayer washes away the ugly feelings, because when humanity touches divinity there is always a transformation. How did David pray for his enemies? He prayed several different ways. One I like is found in Psalm 35:1-5. He says,

> Plead my cause, O Lord, with them that strive with me: fight against them that fight against me. Take hold of shield and buckler, and stand up for mine help. Draw out also the spear, and stop the way against them that persecute me: say unto my soul, I am thy salvation. Let them be confounded and put to shame that seek after my soul: let them be turned back and brought to confusion that devise my hurt. Let them be as chaff before the wind: and let the angel of the Lord chase them.

He was not praying much blessing, but he was praying his heart, and that is the first approach to God. God hears your heart more than your words sometimes. Pray your heart and then ask the Lord to create in you a clean heart and a right spirit, such as David prayed. "Create in me a clean heart, O

God; and renew a right spirit within me. Cast me not away from thy presence; and take not thy holy spirit from me. Restore unto me the joy of thy salvation; and uphold me with thy free spirit" (Psalm 51:10-12).

Peter talks about **blessing** others. Jesus said in Matthew 5 it was the way to live. I Peter 3:8-17 talks not only about blessing, but about being falsely accused.

> Finally, be ye all of one mind, having compassion one of another, love as brethren, be pitiful, be courteous: Not rendering evil for evil, or railing for railing: but contrariwise blessing; knowing that ye are thereunto called, that ye should inherit a blessing. For he that will love life, and see good days, let him refrain his tongue from evil, and his lips that they speak no guile: Let him eschew evil, and do good; let him seek peace, and ensue it. For the eyes of the Lord are over the righteous, and his ears are open unto their prayers; but the face of the Lord is against them that do evil. And who is he that will harm you, if ye be followers of that which is good? But and if ye suffer for righteousness' sake, happy are ye: and be not afraid of their terror, neither be troubled; But sanctify the Lord God in your hearts: and be ready always to give an answer to every man that asketh you a reason of the hope that is in you with meekness and fear: Having a good conscience; that, whereas they speak evil of you, as of evildoers, they may be ashamed that falsely accuse your good conversation in Christ. For it is better, if the will of God be so, that ye suffer for well doing, than for evil doing.

THE BLESSING OF THE PRISON

The Apostle Peter intimates that sometimes the will of God is for a person to suffer for well doing. The important thing is that it be for well doing and not for evil doing. He further states that when this happens it is important to be happy, to not fear, nor be troubled, but have a good conscience and seek to do right.

Charles Wesley, who was conducting one of his many open-air meetings near Killyleagh, Ireland, did what Peter said to do. While he was preaching, a number of persons who disagreed with him rose up against him and assaulted him. Unable to withstand the mob, Wesley fled for his life.

He took refuge in a farmhouse nearby where Jane Moore hid the distraught preacher in the milkhouse. At the same time, his assailants rushed up and she tried to divert their attention by preparing them refreshments. Afraid that they might search the premises and discover Mr. Wesley, she went to the milkhouse on the pretext of getting milk for the angry men.

She told him to go through the rear window and hide under the hedge. He climbed through the window and found a little brook flowing beside the hedge, forming a pool with overhanging branches that gave him a safe retreat. While waiting for the Irishmen to leave, Wesley pulled a pencil and paper from his pocket and wrote the hymn, *Jesus, Lover of My Soul*:

> Jesus, lover of my soul,
> Let me to Thy bosom fly.
> Other refuge have I none,
> Hangs my helpless soul on Thee.

Dr. George Duffield, author of *Stand Up For Jesus*, said, "If there is anything in Christian experience of joy and sorrow,

Prison of False Accusations

of affliction and prosperity, of life and death—that hymn truly is the hymn of the ages." 4

When you are thrown into the prison of false accusation, do not be guilty of becoming like one of your accusers by holding iniquity and hate in your heart. It will pollute you more than it will the accuser. As many have done through the ages, when you are falsely accused, just keep doing what you are doing until it is done, in order to refute the criticism, and learn to keep silent, not fighting back. Also bless, pray, do good and love in the face of criticism and false accusations. Do not let those that seek your hurt bring you down to their level. Keep a pure conscience before the Lord and others and let something good and beautiful come out of your trial!

Yes, something good can come out of the prison experience if you will let it, just as it did for the family of Benjamin Flower. "Benjamin Flower was an English journalist. Some considered him too radical for his times. He was imprisoned for six months. An English girl, whom he later married, frequently visited him in prison. Their daughter was Sarah Flower. She was brilliant and had varied talents. Because of poor health, she dismissed all thoughts of a career she had long dreamed about. She began to write. In the field of writing she gained her greatest achievement. The hymn, *Nearer, My God, to Thee*, will immortalize her as long as time lasts." 5

The false accusations and circumstances that surrounded her family, which caused pain and distress, resulted not in bitterness, but in blessing. Her cross became a glory when her lack became her strength. She could have never written the beautiful words of this hymn had she not suffered in the private chambers of her heart.

THE BLESSING OF THE PRISON

"Out of suffering have emerged the strongest souls."

—Edwin Hubbel Chapin

THE BLESSING OF THE PRISON

5

PRISON OF SUFFERING

Recently when our son Nathaniel, who is a minister, was going through a time of suffering and trial, he received a letter from Rev. Billy Cole, a former missionary to Thailand and other countries. An excerpt from that letter reads as follows: "You cannot reach for the ministry you are reaching for without much struggle and suffering. It just must be. If God would give to you the things you want without much suffering, the gifts of God would consume you like a piece of paper in a hot fire."

The letter came in the mail while I was working on this book. Early one morning, I was awakened with the above excerpt going over and over in my mind. As I prayed and mulled over this thought, it seemed that the Lord wanted me to add this chapter. Then my mind went to Joseph once more. It was the Lord who allowed him to suffer through the pain, false accusations and rejection, but there was a higher purpose than the pain. It was to prepare him for greater things.

Suffering burns out the dross and takes away pride and attitudes that would cause a person to self-destruct. Suffering is as much a part of a Christian's walk as is the resurrection. Paul said to know Christ involved suffering. He said, "That I might know him, and the power of his resurrection, and the fellowship of his sufferings, being made conformable unto his death" (Philippians 3:10).

Suffering is the furnace that makes one more like Christ. Isaiah 48:10 says, "Behold, I have refined thee, but not with silver; I have chosen thee in the furnace of affliction." God did not refine with blessings of gold and silver, but with the hot breath of the furnace of affliction. This is the *needy* stage. A person is made aware of his need of the Lord when the fiery trial burns the hottest. That is when God can mold and make him the way He wants him to be.

"A visitor was watching a silversmith heating the silver in his crucible. Hotter and hotter grew the fires. All the while the smith was closely scanning the crucible. Presently the visitor said, 'Why do you watch the silver so closely? What are you looking for?' 'I am looking for my face,' was the answer. 'When I see my own image in the silver, then I stop. The work is done.' " [1]

It is essential that a Christian must suffer if he wants to reign with Christ. Paul writes,

> And if children, then heirs; heirs of God, and joint-heirs with Christ; if so be that we suffer with him, that we may be also glorified together. For I reckon that the sufferings of this

Prison of Suffering

present time are not worthy to be compared with the glory which shall be revealed in us (Romans 8:17-18).

If you will keep a humble spirit of faith and trust in the Lord during your times of suffering, then you will be properly prepared. God has His reasons for allowing you to go through pain. You may not always understand at the time, but He knows what He is doing.

A person is *tried* basically by five things: God, Satan, the flesh, people, and circumstances. Usually when a person is tried, suffering accompanies the time of trial. The greatest thing you can do during a trial is to keep your integrity with God and to retain faith and trust until the storm passes over, or until the plan of God has been perfected.

Job went through a trial because God orchestrated it. God said to Satan, "Hast thou considered my servant Job, that there is none like him in the earth" (Job 1:8). The result of this question was a release of Job into Satan's hands. "And the Lord said unto Satan, Behold, all that he hath is in thy power; only upon himself put not forth thine hand. So Satan went forth from the presence of the Lord" (Job 1:12). Job's problems escalated so fast that, in one day, he lost everything. This definitely was a trial of his faith. But this was not enough.

After seeing that Job would not curse God to His face, Satan told the Lord the reason why Job would not curse Him was because Job still was well in body. So the Lord said unto Satan, "Behold he is in thine hand; but save his life. So went Satan forth from the presence of the Lord, and smote Job with sore boils from the sole of his foot unto his crown" (Job 2:6-7). Satan gave him the putrid boils and caused him to suffer, but

THE BLESSING OF THE PRISON

God allowed it to happen. We may never understand why God allowed this, but He had a reason and He makes no mistakes.

With Joseph it was different. We know why he was allowed to suffer. Psalm 105:19 says that the word of the Lord tried Joseph. God was preparing Joseph to rule over the land, next in command to the king, and the only way He could get him there was the path that He mapped out for him. Why Joseph had to suffer emotional pain, rejection and false accusations that put him into prison is a clear-cut picture to us, although it was not for Joseph. Joseph did not choose to be tried, nor did he put himself into the trial. God chose to try and prepare him and allowed his brethren and those he loved and respected to bring this about.

Peter talks about suffering in the fourth chapter of his first epistle. He begins with, "Forasmuch then as Christ hath suffered for us in the flesh, arm yourselves likewise with the same mind" (I Peter 4:1). He then ends the chapter with this same vein of thought. Beginning at verse 12 he writes under the inspiration of the Holy Ghost,

> Beloved, think it not strange concerning the fiery trial which is to try you, as though some strange thing happened unto you: But rejoice, inasmuch as ye are partakers of Christ's sufferings; that, when his glory shall be revealed, ye may be glad also with exceeding joy (I Peter 4:12-13).

Peter goes on to contrast the shameful reproach suffered by an evildoer with the honorable reproach suffered by a follower of Christ, then says,

Yet if any man suffer as a Christian, let him not be ashamed; but let him glorify God on this behalf...Wherefore let them that suffer according to the will of God commit the keeping of their souls to him in well doing, as unto a faithful Creator (I Peter 4:16,19).

Paul speaks also about suffering. He writes, "If we suffer, we shall also reign with him" (II Timothy 2:12). Paul suffered many things because of the gospel's sake. "Of the Jews five times received I forty stripes save one. Thrice was I beaten with rods, once was I started, thrice I suffered shipwreck, a night and a day I have been in the deep" (II Corinthians 11:24-25). Hell knew Paul well (Acts 19:15) and because of that knowledge, he became a target for Satan.

The proper example of suffering was our Lord Jesus Christ. Peter writes,

> For even hereunto were ye called: because Christ also suffered for us, leaving us an example, that ye should follow his steps: Who did no sin, neither was guile found in his mouth: Who, when he was reviled, reviled not again; when he suffered, he threatened not; but committed himself to him that judgeth righteously (I Peter 2:21-24).

Two key phrases to notice are: *follow his steps* and *when he suffered he threatened not*, but committed himself to God. When God allows you to walk through times of suffering—whether it be as Paul, who suffered physical torture for the gospel's sake, false accusations against him, and vindictiveness from those that hated him, or as Joseph and the many others who have committed themselves to the Lord's

THE BLESSING OF THE PRISON

service—the two things that are important are to follow in the steps of Christ and commit all things into His hands.

There is a startling statement found in the book of Hebrews. These particular scriptures are talking about the Lord Jesus while He walked on earth. They say, "Though he were a Son, yet learned he obedience by the things which he suffered, and being made perfect, he became the author of eternal salvation unto all them that obey him" (Hebrews 5:8-9).

In looking at these scriptures the question is raised, "Is it possible that if He had not suffered, would He have been obedient?" It must be understood that God was made flesh and dwelt among us (John 1:1,14), but He did not come as a Spirit. "God is a Spirit: and they that worship him must worship him in spirit and in truth" (John 4:24). There had to be a blood sacrifice, so God robed himself in flesh and became God-man; therefore, the human element was that which needed to be brought under subjection to the higher will of God. That is why Jesus prayed in the garden of Gethsemane, "Father, if thou be willing, remove this cup from me: nevertheless not my will, but thine, be done" (Luke 22:42). Hebrews 5:7 says, "Who in the days of his flesh, when he had offered up prayers and supplications with strong crying and tears unto him that was able to save him from death, and was heard in that he feared."

Thus obedience comes through suffering, and that often involves going through things you would rather not go through. It involves walking pathways that you would rather not walk. If your flesh had its way, there would be no tears, no pain, no suffering or sorrow. Dr. Edward T. Sullivan explains it like this:

> And the twelve gates were twelve pearls...every gate a pearl! Every entrance into the heavenly life is through a

pearl! What is a pearl? A wound is made in a shell. A grain of sand, perhaps, gets imbedded in the wound. And all the resources of repair are rushed to the place where the breach has been made. When the breach has been closed, and the process of repair is complete, a pearl is found closing the wound. The break calls forth unsuspected resources of the shell and a beauty appears that is not otherwise brought out. A pearl is a healed wound. No wound, no pearl! [2]

There is a beauty that comes only from suffering. Pain washes away pride, barriers are broken down, falseness collapses, and man is faced with the real issues of life. Years ago the Rev. Hugh Macmillan shared his thoughts how a cross becomes a crown. He said,

> One September in an afternoon walk on the shore of Loch Awe, I saw an aspen tree that reminded me of the burning bush of the desert. Its foliage was one blaze of the most vivid scarlet. I never saw such a wonderful display of color. The leaves were not dead like the usual sere leaves of autumn; they were, on the contrary, quite fresh and full of life. I drew nearer to see the cause of this strange transformation, why the bush burned and was not consumed, and I found that the tree grew on a little mound, from which the waters of a rill that existed only in rainy weather had washed away the soil, leaving the roots to a large extent exposed. The conditions of life were thus unfavorable; but instead of being made less beautiful, it became more beautiful in consequence. The poverty of its soil had changed the ordinary dill green of its leaves into the

most brilliant red, as if each separate leaf were a flame in the heart of a furnace.

A soft breeze of evening whispered through the trembling, fiery tongues of the transfigured aspen, and in my awe-stricken soul I heard the still small voice as of old from the burning bush, telling me that thus it is with human life, from which the stream of circumstances washes away all its worldly good things in which it trusted, leaving its roots bare and exposed. God's breath kindles in it a beauty unknown before, which no mere prosperous worldly condition could have developed; and the poverty and sorrowfulness of its state, only make it glow with the light of heaven, and its cross becomes its crown. [3]

It is hard to walk through suffering and distresses, but we know that Christ gives victory over suffering. Christ offers His constantly abiding presence during the most difficult times. The basis of it all is not to make man feel pain, but that the finer things of life and the greatness of God are to be revealed more clearly. The wonderful thing about it all is that the Lord Jesus promised to send back a comforter and before ascending into glory, He said, "Lo, I am with you alway, even unto the end of the world" (Matthew 28:20).

Pennyfather, an author in the early 1900's, wrote,

Suffering is a very solitary thing. Great suffering brings upon the heart a sense of loneliness, and it needs all that God Himself can be to the stricken one. It might seem almost impossible that anything more than the peace of God could be promised, but there is a fuller promise yet. "The God of Peace shall be with you." Here language is exhausted. The portion of every praying one is "the peace of God," and when even that is not enough, "the God of Peace," Himself Emmanuel, stands beside you. [4]

Sometimes God allows people to suffer so they can help other people gain victory through their time of suffering. Spurgeon once told of how he was utterly depressed in spirit and soul, discouraged, and failing in health. Just before leaving for a recuperation, he preached about the cry, "My God, my God, why hast thou forsaken me?" The experience was so sad that he wished it would never happen again.

Afterwards a man came to see him and Spurgeon describes him as being one step away from an insane asylum. He told Spurgeon that after hearing his sermon, he felt that Spurgeon was the only one who could understand him. Spurgeon helped him as best he could.

After five years Spurgeon finally saw the man at a lecture he was giving at a college. He was a completely changed man. Spurgeon said he was willing to undergo hundreds of such experiences now that he knew God permitted it to happen so that he could know and sympathize with people under similar predicaments.

Do not look at suffering as a time of wasted motion, but use it to gain insight into the things of God and realize that when you suffer, you will be able to help someone else in need. What *you* feel or experience always prepares you more than just observing how someone else feels.

The psalmist wrote, "It is good for me that I have been afflicted: that I might learn thy statutes" (Psalm 119:71).

THE BLESSING OF THE PRISON

"Calamity is the perfect glass wherein we truly see and know ourselves."

—William Davenant

THE BLESSING OF THE PRISON

6

PRISON OF TROUBLE

Eliphaz said to Job when Job was covered with boils from head to toe and had lost everything, "Yet man is born for trouble" (Job 5:7). This is not a comforting thought, and one that is debatable. One thing we do know is that when trouble comes, the Lord has promised to be with His children.

Although life has many joyous moments, exhilarating pleasures, and other wonderful experiences, it also has troubles. Life is not easy, nor should it be. If all went well, if everything was sunshine, life would become a desert. There must be the rains and the wind to clean and renew. Beecher wrote, "There is but one easy place in this world, and that is the grave."

Trouble brought on by other people leaves less of a troubled spirit in the inner man than trouble that is brought on by self. When you know you are doing right, then you can handle things

THE BLESSING OF THE PRISON

a whole lot better than if you know you caused it by your own wrong doings. Trouble comes several ways:

1. You can bring trouble on yourself by disobedience. This was proven by the story of Achan (Joshua 6:18; 7:1). The story of Jonah substantiates this. God told Jonah to do one thing; he did the opposite. Jonah's words, in the belly of the great fish the Lord prepared for him, described his trouble as *"hell."* He said, "I cried by reason of mine affliction unto the Lord, and he heard me; out of the belly of hell cried I, and thou heardest my voice" (Jonah 2:2). The Lord will always help those who humble themselves and cry unto Him in their time of self-inflicted trouble.

2. Some people get thrown into prison because of their own actions. It is the consequence of sin. "A painter once wanted a picture of innocence. He found and painted a little child kneeling beside his mother at prayer. The palms of his hands were reverently folded, mild blue eyes upturned with an expression of devotion and peace. The painter prized this portrait of young Rupert above all else and hung it prominently in his study, calling it *Innocence*.

"Years later when the artist was old, the portrait was still there. He had often thought of painting a counterpart, the picture of guilt. One day he purposely visited a neighboring prison. On the damp floor of the cell lay a wretched man, named Rupert, heavily ironed. His body was horribly wasted, his eyes hollow, vice sprouted all over his face. The old painter succeeded admirably, and the portraits hung side by side—*Innocence* and *Guilt*." [1]

3. Your *mouth* can get you into trouble. Judges 11:30-35 tells of a rash vow made by Jephthah. His own words indicted him. "And it came to pass, when he saw her, that he rent his clothes, and said, Alas, my daughter! thou hast brought me very low, and thou art one of them that trouble me: for I have *opened my mouth* unto the Lord, and I cannot go back" (Judges 11:35).

4. God can send trouble because of your disrespect for the man of God, rebellion against the Word of God, or for blaming others instead of repenting when confronted with a wrong. This happened to Saul (I Samuel 15:16-35). "But the Spirit of the Lord departed from Saul, and an evil spirit from the Lord *troubled* him" (I Samuel 16:14).

5. Bitterness can trouble you. Hebrews 12:14-15 gives instructions on how to live with people. It does not give room for offenses and hurts. It says, "Follow peace with all men, and holiness, without which no man shall see the Lord: Looking diligently lest any man fail of the grace of God; lest any root of bitterness springing up trouble you, and thereby many be defiled."

6. Satan will send trouble as he did in Job 1-2. "And the Lord said unto Satan, Behold, he is in thine hand; but save his life. So went Satan forth from the presence of the Lord, and smote Job with sore boils from the sole of his foot unto his crown" (Job 2:6-7). It was not God that put boils on Job, it was Satan, and he is constantly trying to bring people down into the depths of despair.

7. People can trouble you because you serve God. "But and if ye suffer for righteousness' sake, happy are ye: and be not afraid of their terror, neither be troubled; For it is better, if the will of God be so, that ye suffer for well doing, than for evil doing" (I Peter 3:14,17).

King Hezekiah brought reform to Jerusalem and cast out all the idols and "wrought that which was good and right and truth

THE BLESSING OF THE PRISON

before the Lord his God. And in every work that he began in the service of the house of God, and in the law, and in the commandments, to seek his God, he did it with all his heart, and prospered" (II Chronicles 31:20-21).

When everything is going well, when there has been a great victory or reformation, look out! The enemy is just around the corner to try and steal it from you. He will always instigate trouble to disturb your mind.

King Sennacherib of Assyria sought to terrify the inhabitants of Jerusalem. He surrounded the city and mocked them, trying to win the people over to his side against their leader, Hezekiah. "Then they cried with a loud voice in the Jews' speech unto the people of Jerusalem that were on the wall, to affright them, and to *trouble* them; that they might take the city" (II Chronicles 32:18).

Hezekiah and the prophet Isaiah prayed and cried to heaven.

> And the Lord sent an angel, which cut off all the mighty men of valour, and the leaders and captains in the camp of the king of Assyria. So he returned with shame of face to his own land. And when he was come into the house of his god, they that came forth of his own bowels slew him there with the sword. Thus the Lord saved Hezekiah and the inhabitants of Jerusalem from the hand of Sennacherib, the king of Assyria, and from the hand of all other, and guided them on every side (II Chronicles 32:20-23).

It does not matter how powerful the enemy is, God is more powerful. The story of the exodus of the children of Israel proves this. When the Israelites went into the midst of the sea upon dry ground, the Egyptians pursued them. The difference was that God was on Israel's side. That makes all the difference in the world.

> And it came to pass, that in the morning watch the Lord looked unto the host of the Egyptians through the pillar of fire and of the cloud, and *troubled* the host of the Egyptians, And took off their chariot wheels, that they drave them heavily: so that the Egyptians said, Let us flee from the face of Israel; for the Lord fighteth for them against the Egyptians (Exodus 14:24-25).

Trouble became the seed-bed for a miracle! If all had gone well, God would not have needed to perform the miracle of parting the sea and then taking off the chariot wheels of the enemy. This story shows that God has a sense of humor. What a way to win a war! No swords, no bullets, just the simple unscrewing of bolts. God has a way of embarrassing the enemy. He does not need much to win because He is so powerful.

Trouble can be a blessing in disguise. "When Lord Clive, as a young man, in the spirit of adventure set out from his British home for India, the ship upon which he sailed was caught in a terrific storm. Continuous adverse gales drove it far off the course, until it finally limped into a South American harbour. There he had to remain for many months before being able to get passage to India.

"But during the long wait he acquired the Portuguese language. This qualified him when he did reach India to take an important position with the East India Company, ultimately resulting in his being appointed by the crown as Governor General of India. Do not deplore the upsets; they may be God's messengers." [2]

THE BLESSING OF THE PRISON

Look upon trouble as a time of seeing God in His glory, or as preparation for greater things! If there was not any trouble, life could easily become an empty bubble. It is the time of trouble that makes God's glory shine in the lives of men and women. The dark times are when His light shines the brightest. He promised to give treasures in the darkness. "I will go before thee, and make the crooked places straight: I will break in pieces the gates of brass, and cut in sunder the bars of iron: and I will give thee the *treasures of darkness*, and hidden riches of secret places" (Isaiah 45:2-3).

The Lord gave special instruction on what to do when trouble came. He gave hope not to the man sitting on top of the world, but to those who were in trouble and to the oppressed. Why did Jesus come? His own words explain it.

> The Spirit of the Lord is upon me, because he hath anointed me to preach the gospel to the poor; he hath sent me to heal the broken-hearted, to preach deliverance to the captives, and recovering of sight to the blind, to set at liberty them that are bruised (Luke 4:18).

It sounds like a group of pretty desperate people. Look what He promises to be or do for those who are in trouble:

A Refuge: "The Lord also will be a refuge for the oppressed, a *refuge* in times of *trouble*" (Psalm 9:9).

An Uplifter: "Have mercy upon me, O Lord; consider my *trouble* which I suffer of them that hate me, thou that *liftest me up* from the gates of death" (Psalm 9:13).

A Rock: "For in the time of *trouble* he shall hide me in his pavilion; in the secret of his tabernacle shall he hide me; he shall set me up upon a rock" (Psalm 27:5).

A Strength: "But the salvation of the righteous is of the Lord: he is their *strength* in the time of *trouble*. And the Lord shall help them, and deliver them: he shall deliver them from the wicked, and save them, because they **trust** in him" (Psalm 37:39-40).

A Present Help: "God is our refuge and strength, a *very present help* in *trouble*" (Psalm 46:1).

A Defense: "But I will sing of thy power; yea, I will sing aloud of thy mercy in the morning: for thou hast been my *defence* and refuge in the day of my *trouble*" (Psalm 59:16).

A Deliverer: "They cried unto the Lord in their *trouble*, and he *delivered* them out of their distresses" (Psalm 107:6).

A Reviver: "Though I walk in the midst of *trouble*, thou wilt *revive* me: thou shalt stretch forth thine hand against the wrath of mine enemies, and thy right hand shall save me" (Psalm 138:7).

When you have hurt, pain, anguish of soul, deep overwhelming grief, non-stop tears and endless sobbing, what should you do? There are several things to do, but a tried and true way is the formula consisting of *prayer, fasting and trust in the Word*. If you study the Scriptures, you will see this formula

THE BLESSING OF THE PRISON

in action over and over. If you will do the following five things, you will reap a victory!

1. **Fast unto the Lord.**
2. **Trust in the Lord.**
3. **Devour the Word of God.**
4. **Pray fervently to God.**
5. **Humble yourself.**

Jehoshaphat found out that this formula works. When he was surrounded by the enemy and threatened by their taunts, he first of all set himself to seek the Lord and proclaimed a **fast** throughout all Judah. Then they all **prayed** and asked help of the Lord. His prayer was,

> O Lord God of our fathers, art not thou God in heaven? and rulest not thou over all the kingdoms of the heathen? and in thine hand is there not power and might, so that none is able to withstand thee?...Now the children of Ammon and Moab and mount Seir, whom thou wouldest not let Israel invade, when they came out of the land of Egypt, but they turned from them, and destroyed them not; Behold, I say, how they reward us, to come to cast us out of thy possession, which thou hast given us to inherit...O our God, wilt thou not judge them? for we have no might against this great company that cometh against us; neither know we what to do: but are eyes are upon thee (II Chronicles 20:6, 10-12).

After they prayed and fasted, the Lord sent them a message. He said, "Ye shall not need to fight in this battle: set yourselves, stand ye still, and see the salvation of the Lord with you, O

Judah and Jerusalem: fear not, nor be dismayed; to morrow go out against them: for the Lord will be with you" (II Chronicles 20:17).

With those powerful words, Jehoshaphat slept a little easier that night. The very people that were coming against him were the ones that Jehoshaphat had treated well. The enemy was returning evil for good, but God was going to have the last say. The next day, Jehoshaphat appointed singers unto the Lord and when they began to sing and praise the Lord, the Lord set ambushments against the enemy and not one of them escaped.

Just as the Lord fought for Jehoshaphat, He will always fight for those who are in the right! If you have trouble because of people who are against you without just cause, do not fear, but rest in the Lord and wait patiently in Him. He is on the side of the righteous and He always wins!

When America was in trouble, Abraham Lincoln wrote an address to the nation during the Civil War that was his proclamation for a national fast-day, by which he did designate and set apart Thursday, April 30, 1863, as a day of national humiliation, fasting, and prayer. Lincoln wrote,

> It is the duty of nations as well as of men to own their dependence upon the overruling power of God; to confess their sins and transgressions in humble sorrow, yet with assured hope that genuine repentance will lead to mercy and pardon; and to recognize the sublime truth announced in the Holy Scriptures and proven by all history, that those nations only are blessed whose God is the Lord.
>
> The awful calamity of civil war which now desolates the land may be but punishment inflicted upon us for our

presumptuous sins, to the needful end of our national reformation as a whole people.

Intoxicated with unbroken success, we have become too self-sufficient to feel the necessity, and too proud to pray to the God that made us. It behooves us, then, to humble ourselves before the offended Power, to confess our national sins, and to pray for clemency and forgiveness. [3]

If you are facing trouble, the greatest thing you can do is to humble yourself and pray. Call on the Lord and He will be with you. "God is our refuge and strength, a very present help in trouble" (Psalm 46:1). He is present, right there with you, during the most painful times of your life.

During one of the most devastating trials of my life, which was caused by other people, I was riding home on an airplane after speaking at a Women's Retreat, and I laid my head on a pillow, turned my face towards the window and cried, saying, "God, it hurts. It hurts! Oh, it hurts. I've never been in a trial like this and the pain and anguish is too deep for words."

I would like to tell you that an angel came and visited me in my deep sorrow, but there was not one visible. There was only the bitterest pain I had ever endured. My soul was exceedingly sorrowful. I had just ministered to many dear women, but I was alone in my suffering, 35,000 feet above the earth.

Suddenly I looked out the window to the right of the airplane and all was dark and gray at dusk, but for a horizontal strip of red. It looked like a pool of blood. As I watched it, it seemed to lengthen and the words of the old song came to my mind, "I see a crimson stream of blood. It flows from Calvary." As I wept it seemed the Lord spoke to me and said, "I came to heal the broken-hearted and to set the captive free. The trial you are in will soon be over and something good will come out of it. Just wait patiently for that appointed time."

I opened my Bible and read Psalm 37. The following phrases are the highlights of that chapter:

> Fret not thyself because of evildoers.
> Trust in the Lord.
> Delight thyself also in the Lord; He shall give thee the desires of thine heart.
> Commit thy way unto the Lord; trust also in him; and he shall bring it to pass.
> Rest in the Lord.
> Wait upon the Lord.

Then I read,

The steps of a good man are ordered by the Lord: and he delighteth in his way. Though he fall, he shall not be utterly cast down: for the Lord upholdeth him with his hand. I have been young, and now am old: yet have I not seen the righteous forsaken, nor his seed begging bread. But the salvation of the righteous is of the Lord: he is their strength in the time of trouble. And the Lord shall help them, and deliver them: he shall deliver them from the wicked, and save them, because they trust in him (Psalm 37:23-25, 39-40).

Beautiful Queen Esther knew the power of calling upon the Lord in the time of trouble. She commanded the Jews to fast and pray when they were threatened by the enemy. "Then Esther bade them return Mordecai this answer, Go, gather to-

THE BLESSING OF THE PRISON

gether all the Jews that are present in Shushan, and fast ye for me, and neither eat nor drink three days, night or day: I also and my maidens will fast likewise" (Esther 4:15-16).

The end of the story is that the enemy was hanged on the very gallows he had prepared for Mordecai. After this incident God allowed Mordecai to be elevated to a new position in the household of the king.

Moses, the great deliverer of the Israelites, was thrown into the prison of trouble when Korah and several men of renown gathered themselves together against Moses and Aaron and said unto them, "Ye take too much upon you, seeing all the congregation are holy, every one of them, and the Lord is among them: wherefore then lift ye up yourselves above the congregation of the Lord?" (Numbers 16:3). Moses immediately fell on his face when he heard this accusation. He then told Korah and his followers to meet at the door of the tabernacle and God would choose who was right.

When they had all gathered together, Moses spoke to them all.

> And Moses said, Hereby ye shall know that the Lord hath sent me to do all these works; for I have not done them of mine own mind. If these men die the common death of all men, or if they be visited after the visitation of all men; then the Lord hath not sent me. But if the Lord make a new thing, and the earth open her mouth, and swallow them up, with all that appertain unto them, and they go down quick into the pit; then ye shall understand that these men have provoked the Lord. And it came to pass, as he had made an end of speaking all these words, that the ground clave asunder that was under them. And the earth opened her

mouth, and swallowed them up, and their houses, and all the men that appertained unto Korah, and all their goods. They, and all that appertained to them, went down alive into the pit, and the earth closed upon them: and they perished from among the congregation (Numbers 16:28-33).

It is a serious thing to make false accusations against the righteous.

If you are in the prison of trouble, this is not the time to curse, seek revenge, or become bitter. It is the time to draw nigh to God, call upon Him and trust in Him. Deliverance will come! Psalm 7:10 says, "My defence is of God, which saveth the upright in heart." It is a promise! Since it is impossible for God to lie, you can stand upon His Word and see the salvation of the Lord.

This happened over and over in Bible days. When King Hezekiah received word from Rabshakeh, the messenger from the king of Assyria, "He rent his clothes, and covered himself with sackcloth, and went into the house of the Lord" (II Kings 19:1). Hezekiah sent word to Isaiah the prophet saying, "Thus saith Hezekiah, This day is a day of trouble...wherefore lift up thy prayer for the remnant that are left" (II Kings 19:4).

Isaiah sent back a very positive answer:

...Thus shall ye say to your master, Thus saith the Lord, Be not afraid of the words which thou hast heard, with which the servants of the king of Assyria have blasphemed me. Behold, I will send a blast upon him, and he shall hear a rumour, and shall return to his own land; and I will cause him to fall by the sword in his own land (II Kings 19:6-7).

THE BLESSING OF THE PRISON

Rabshakeh did not scare easily. He kept coming back to taunt the people of Hezekiah's kingdom. He came back and said to them, "Let not thy God in whom thou trustest deceive thee, saying, Jerusalem shall not be delivered into the hand of the king of Assyria" (II Kings 19:10). It is apparent that Rabshakeh did not know who he was dealing with, or he never would have spoken against God in such a derogatory fashion.

As always, God let them talk, scheme, and plan, but He got in the last word. The end of all the talk back and forth between Rabshakeh and Hezekiah resulted in a massacre.

> And it came to pass that night, that the angel of the Lord went out, and smote in the camp of the Assyrians an hundred fourscore and five thousand: and when they arose early in the morning, behold, they were all dead corpses. So Sennacherib king of Assyria departed, and went and returned, and dwelt at Nineveh. And it came to pass, as he was worshipping in the house of Nisroch his god, that Adrammelech and Sharezer his sons smote him with the sword (II Kings 19:35-37).

It does not matter what you are going through. If you will do as Hezekiah did, the Lord will come to your rescue and help you. The end will be victory for you, even if it seems like all evil is scheming against you. King Hezekiah did not go to the house of the Lord *once*, he went several times. "And Hezekiah received the letter of the hand of the messengers, and read it: and Hezekiah went up into the house of the Lord, and spread it before the Lord" (II Kings 19:14).

When life is seemingly going great, and suddenly trouble comes into your life, it is difficult to understand that something good can come out of it. When Thomas Nast, an artist, once gave a public exhibition of his skill, he did a strange thing. He painted a beautiful landscape with fields of grain, a farmhouse, green meadows and an orchard. When he finished the audience applauded.

Then he took some darker colors, stepped to the canvas once more and applied them recklessly to the canvas. Out went the bright sky. He blotted out the meadows, fields, orchards and buildings. Up, down and across passed the artist's hand until the landscape was totally obliterated, and nothing but a drab picture remained. He stepped back and said, "It is finished." The audience looked at it in puzzlement without any applause.

The artist then ordered his attendants to place a gold frame around the ruined work of art, and to turn it to a vertical position. Before the audience there stood a panel picture of a beautiful waterfall, the water plunging over a precipice of dark rock, surrounded by trees. After seeing the transformation, the audience burst into applause.

It may look like the Lord has allowed your life to be colored with dark, drab colors and the beautiful picture of your life has been ruined, but He never ruins anything; He only makes things better. Trust in Him and be not afraid for He does all things well and will be with you through the darkest night. The sun will shine again and you will see the rainbow after the storm.

THE BLESSING OF THE PRISON

"There can be no rainbow without a cloud and a storm."

—J.H. Vincent

THE BLESSING OF THE PRISON

7

ATTITUDE MAKES THE DIFFERENCE

There are several attitudes that are important to have when one enters into a prison experience. It is not enough to know what to do, but it is important to put that knowledge into practice.

How you face trouble will determine the outcome. Stephenson said, "You cannot run away from a weakness; you must some time fight it out or perish; and if that be so, why not now, and where you stand?" [1] It is the same with the difficulties of life. You cannot run from them; you must face them with courage, bravery, and dignity.

You must realize who is *really* in charge of your life. If God is in charge and you are walking according to His Word to the best of your ability, then He will let happen to You only that which He considers to be best for you. If you can live with this

THE BLESSING OF THE PRISON

knowledge in your heart, you can be like the little grandmother who was unafraid during an earthquake several years ago. The inhabitants of a small village were very alarmed, but she was surprisingly calm and joyous.

At length, one of them said to her, "Mother, are you not afraid?"

She said, "No, I rejoice to know that I serve a God who has the power to shake the world."

Your world may be shaking and in a big upheaval, but be not afraid, God is in charge!

How you perceive or see things is most important.

It is not what happens to you that matters most, it is your attitude about it.

When a young salesman had been out less than a month, he was so discouraged that he was about to give up. Just then he encountered a man who had been on the road for years.

"Well, how is the selling game going?" asked the older man.

"Pretty poor," answered the youngster. "I've been insulted at nearly every place I have visited."

"That's strange," said the old timer. "I've been on the road forty years. I've had my samples flung into the street, I've been taken by the scruff of the neck and hurled downstairs. I've had doors slammed in my face time and time again, and I can't tell you the number of times I've been cursed. I'll even admit that I've been rolled in the gutter. But in all the years of my selling I can't remember ever having been insulted once."

La Rochefoulcauld said, "Little minds are too much wounded by little things; great minds see all, and are not even hurt." [2]

He had learned to see that which was important and to ignore that which was not.

Attitude Makes the Difference

The story has been told about the young girl who lived with her husband on an Indian reservation where he was stationed during his time of training. She wrote home to her father that she was coming home because she could not stand the dirt and the differences in culture, etc. Her father wrote back two lines which changed her life. He wrote: "Two men behind prison bars: One looked out and saw the mud, the other looked out and saw the stars."

She said, "All I was seeing was the mud or the negative." She started learning the Indian language, how to cook Indian breads and stews, how to make ponchos, and to do other interesting things. When it was time for her husband to leave, she cried because she did not want to go. The question is: What changed? It was her attitude.

When Elisha was at Dothan, his servant went out for a morning walk and saw that they were surrounded by the enemy. He immediately was seized with an *attitude or spirit of fear*, because he perceived incorrectly. When his master, Elisha, sensed his fear, he stayed relaxed because He knew that God was bigger than the enemy. He prayed, "Lord, I pray thee, open his eyes, that he may see" (II Kings 6:17). When his eyes were opened, he saw how things really were. It was not as bad as it looked. The mountain was full of horses and chariots of fire round about Elisha. God had not forgotten them during their time of trouble. As He was with Elisha, He will be with you also!

Living right all the time, whether in the prison or not, is very important. The following poem entitled, *The Hundredth Man,* written by Dr. Frank Crane, explains this principle.

The hundredth man is the man who is earning his wage.

He is doing just about what he ought to do, barring the universal human frailties.

He is making good.

When he makes an appointment he keeps it.

When he has to deliver "a message to Garcia," he delivers it. He does not explain why he couldn't.

When he states a thing it is just about as he states it; no more, no less.

He does not exaggerate, gesticulate, nor vociferate. As a consequence his ordinary tone of voice is more convincing than other men's shouting.

He is not fond of the pronoun I.

He does not indulge in self-dispraise, that most disagreeable fashion of self-praise.

He is much more concerned about the right than about his rights.

He shoulders cheerfully his responsibilities.

He gives to the world an equivalent for what he gets from the world.

Wherever you find a man of this kind you find ninety-nine who are hanging on to his coattails.

It is the one man out of every hundred that is making things go: the others are following along.

The hundredth man is not looking for favors, tips, pulls and help.

In any business he is the one who is indispensable. For whatever he does he does a little better than anyone else could do it.

He is dependable. You never have to watch him to see whether he is doing what he is supposed to do or not.

He is a good loser. When he makes mistakes he owns up and takes the consequences.

He despises no human being.

He respects every woman.

He demands nothing from his friends.

He is never mean, small, selfish, vindictive, nor sulky.

When he feels bad he goes away until he gets over it, and does not afflict other people with his depression.

He knows the golden mean. For he is courteous without being obsequious; kind, but not patronizing; strong, but not coarse; gentle, but not effeminate; firm, but not stubborn; self-respecting, but not an egotist; decent, but not prudish; human, but not animal; loving, but not sentimental; careful, but not timid; appreciative, but not effusive; cheerful and optimistic, but not oppressively so.

And everybody thinks he's the hundredth man—except himself. [3]

Paul exemplified this principle well. He was falsely accused many times. He was accused of being an Egyptian leader who had murdered 4,000 people (Acts 21:38). He was accused of being mad (Acts 26:24). He was accused of many things which they could not prove (Acts 25:7). Did this affect Paul's daily life? No! He continued steadfastly in doing that which the Lord had called him to do. When the false accusers had him thrown in prison, he continued to do that which was right before God. It was said of him that the guards had to be changed every four hours because Paul's intense zeal and love for the truth would cause them to be converted to Christ. Nothing made Paul bitter against God or caused him to stop doing what he was doing. He just kept pressing on towards the mark.

THE BLESSING OF THE PRISON

The person who makes it out of any prison he is cast into will be a person that does not let anger toward his betrayer control him. An anonymous author shares the following insight about the brutality of anger.

> There is no form of savagery so manifest as anger. Nothing is more uncalled for, accomplishes less good nor makes people more unhappy than the curse of a bad temper. Nothing was ever accomplished by it except blighting the flowers of the human heart and poisoning its springs. It is the brutal expression of supreme selfishness. No gentleman will ever stoop to the vulgarity of anger. It is an unnecessary attack of temporary insanity that is damaging not only to the mental powers by the physical as well.
>
> Physical culture chemists have demonstrated in their laboratories that there is a poison secreted in the body, when one is angry, that is very harmful. It interrupts the digestion, disorganizes the whole alimentary canal, upsets the nerves, dethrones the mind and irritates the whole body. It is positively a shortener of life.
>
> Anger should not only be considered coarse and vulgar, but a positive menace to all physical power.
>
> It is so sweet to be kind and tender; it is so constructive to be quiet; it is so worthwhile to be thoughtful of others that one's life can be prepared for service in no finer way than by perfect mastery of the human spirit. [4]

Joseph's integrity kept him from this brutal anger. When Joseph was testing his brothers to see if they were still cold and callused, he put his cup into Benjamin's sack of grain. This brought them back to the palace where they begged for mercy.

Joseph told them that whoever had the cup in his sack would be his servant. At this point, "...Judah came near unto him, and said, Oh my lord, let thy servant, I pray thee, speak a word in my lord's ears, and let not thine anger burn against thy servant: for thou art even as Pharaoh" (Genesis 44:18).

Joseph could have been filled with anger and sought vengeance, but instead he wept when he saw that his brothers had changed. He could contain himself no longer and put everyone out of the room and identified himself to his brothers, where he fell on their necks and embraced them with tears and forgiveness.

The attitude of forgiveness is imperative! Forgiveness is letting a person that did you wrong back into your good graces. It is forgetting what he did and allowing him to have another chance. "To err is human. To forgive is divine." Joseph's brothers did not deserve to be forgiven, but Joseph forgave.

Those that tormented Jesus did not deserve forgiveness, but He forgave. He forgave them for spitting at Him, mocking Him, falsely accusing Him, and torturing Him. While in the deepest pain He cried, "Father, forgive them for they know not what they do!"

Two attitudes come into focus here. Pride fights back in the flesh. Humility wars in the Spirit. Pride gossips, concocts and imagines evil, and threatens using fear tactics. Humility repents, prays, fasts, reads the Word and speaks the Word instead of cursing. Prides hates and vindicates. Humility says, "The Lord will take care of me." Pride will not forgive. Humility forgives and does not get even.

The Lord retreats from the proud but He draws nigh to the humble. "God resisteth the proud, but giveth grace unto the humble" (James 4:7). During the reign of King Josiah, there came a time when the Word of the Lord came to him and it caused him to tremble. "And it came to pass, when the king had heard the words of the law, that he rent his clothes" (II Chronicles 34:19). The result?

> Because thine heart was tender, and thou didst humble thyself before God, when thou heardest his words against this place, and against the inhabitants thereof, and humbledst thyself before me, and didst rend thy clothes, and weep before me; I have even heard thee also, saith the Lord (II Chronicles 34:27).

Keep an attitude of integrity, caring more what God thinks than what man thinks. Joseph's brothers were deceitful. They lied to their father and hatched one of the biggest deceptions of all time. They cared only about their own interests and did not care that they had broken their father's heart or their brother's heart. *Deceitfulness* is an ugly word. It screams of treachery, lies and hurtful schemes.

In spite of the deceit that surrounded Joseph, he kept his integrity with God. Whereas his brothers lied, he refused to lie. He would not succumb to peer pressure or even the pattern of blood relations. He cared more about doing right than being free.

Have an attitude of courage. No matter what you encounter *be of good courage!* Things will get better. Take the words that the Lord spoke to Moses and apply them to your situation: "Be strong and of a good courage, fear not, nor be afraid of them: for the Lord thy God, he it is that doth go with thee; he will not fail thee, nor forsake thee" (Deuteronomy

31:6). Face it with bravery, determining to do right no matter what!

Still dream! Still care! Do not let the *killer* attitude of your tormentors put out your light of love. In November 1994, while working on this book, I received a letter from a friend in Arkansas with the following reading that she wanted to share with me. It portrays the *meanness* of some people and the *gentleness* of other people. You can either have the scorpion attitude or you can choose to have the loving attitude of the man who cared.

> A missionary walked along the Ganges River. A sight which was most unusual caught his attention. An elderly man sitting on the river bank spied a piece of driftwood to which clung a scorpion. Realizing the inability of scorpions to swim, the old man reached out to catch the floating wood. The scorpion struck its treacherous blow. With a gasp of pain, the man yanked his hand back. But then, to the missionary's amazement, the man reached out again and repeatedly, each time experiencing the scorpion's deadly reaction. Finally the missionary could restrain himself no longer. "Let the scorpion die...save yourself! Look at your bloodied, swollen hand. That creature is killing you!" The old man shook his head and softly replied, "I cannot allow the nature of the scorpion to kill destroy my nature to save."

Do not let your nature to care be destroyed by lesser good! Many times jealousy is at the core of the *scorpion* nature. "Jealousy is cruel as the grave: the coals thereof are coals of fire, which hath a most vehement flame" (Song of Solomon 8:6). Jealously is a killer! It has a hot, fiery breath with flames

THE BLESSING OF THE PRISON

of hate, lies or shaded half-truths which belch from the mouth of a person who has been inflicted with the nature of Satan. Lucifer was jealous of the glory the Lord God received and wanted to exalt his throne above the Lord's. His proud nature could not stand the exaltation of God. The same spirit can get inside a man who lets jealously become the scepter that rules his life.

It is important to have an attitude of surrender, not of resistance, toward the Lord's dealings and His plans. If you have the assurance that you are God's child, then you must believe that the steps of a good man are *ordered by the Lord!* If He orders them, then He will order the outcome. It does not matter how Satan, or even the brethren or sisters, scheme against you. God has you in His sight. He knows where you are and He cares about you. That does not mean you will not walk through pain and suffering or experience trouble. He uses these things to prepare you for greater things. He will not let anything come upon you that He does not feel you can bear. "There hath no temptation taken you but such as is common to man: but God is faithful, who will not suffer you to be tempted above that ye are able; but will with the temptation also make a way to escape, that ye may be able to bear it" (I Corinthians 10:13).

You are not alone in your sorrow; others have felt the same pain. Among the parables that Chinese teachers use is the story of a woman who lost an only son. She was grief-stricken and made her sorrow a wailing wall. She finally went to a wise old philosopher who told her, "I will give you back your son if you will bring me some mustard seed. However, the seed must come from a home where there has never been any sorrow." Eagerly she started her search, and went from house to house. In every case she learned that a loved one had been lost. "How selfish I have been in my grief," she said, "sorrow is common to all."

The key is *how* you deal with it. It can either be a stepping stone to God or a stumblingblock to failure. You can either learn, grow and become what God is trying to make out of you, or you can resist God and shrivel up and die.

A note of caution is necessary here. Be careful of what you say to yourself or to others when there is a call of God involved.

"Dr. W. Leon Tucker told this amazing incident: Dr. Percival, a busy surgeon, was a Christian. He had one daughter, Kitty, whom he loved devotedly. One day she came to her father and told him she was going as a missionary to China. He said, 'Kitty, I forbid you ever to get out of my sight.' At last she gave up plans for going, and married. She had two darling children.

"I lived next door to Dr. Percival. One day he told me that he had to give up his surgeon's license because of the condition of his eyes. Later he had to have an operation on his eyes. When the bandages were taken from them, his doctor said, 'In two weeks you will be totally blind.'

"Dr. Percival sent for Kitty and the babies to come. He carefully felt their faces and seemed to get a mental picture of them in his fingertips. He took me out into the light to 'look at his pastor.' It was a sad day in our block, and everyone was weeping.

"Months later I went out to lunch with Dr. Percival. I had to help feed him. As he walked home I could see that he wanted to say something. 'Say it, Doctor,' I said. 'Dr. Tucker,' he said, 'do you think God is retributive?' I told him I did not believe it. He said, 'Tucker, I told Kitty that she could never go out of my

THE BLESSING OF THE PRISON

sight, but God has taken her from my sight. Wherever you go, plead with parents to keep out of the way when God calls their children into His service.'" [5]

It is best to surrender and follow God's leading than to resist His plan. The attitude of the ten spies in Numbers 13 was to resist the perfect plan of God. As a result they all met death instead of enjoying the promised land, whereas Joshua and Caleb received the blessing of the promised land and became powerful leaders.

> And the men, which Moses sent to search the land, who returned, and made all the congregation to murmur against him, by bringing up a slander upon the land, Even those men that did bring up the evil report upon the land, died by the plague before the Lord (Numbers 14:36-37).

This is not saying that all bad things that happen are the judgments of God. No, a thousand times, No! It is only food for thought to help you be careful of how you act and what you say during a time of preparation for a call, a prison experience, or times of pain. Surrender is always better than resistance.

"Earth has no sorrow that heaven cannot heal."

—Thomas Moore

THE BLESSING OF THE PRISON

8

PRAYER IN THE PRISON

*J*esus was in the garden of Gethsemane and had prayed His agonizing prayer. He then went to where Peter, James, and John were. When He saw them sleeping He spoke to them words that apply to every Christian. He said them during one of His greatest trials. They were simply, "Watch and pray, that ye enter not into temptation: the spirit indeed is willing, but the flesh is weak" (Matthew 26:41).

Peter echoed those same words in I Peter 4:7. "But the end of all things is at hand: be ye therefore sober, and watch unto prayer." What does it mean to watch? *Watch* means "to wait patiently." The following Scriptures instruct the righteous to be at peace and become better acquainted with the Lord while waiting in prayer.

THE BLESSING OF THE PRISON

> Rest in the Lord, and wait patiently for him (Psalm 37:7).
>
> Acquaint now thyself with him, and be at peace: thereby good shall come unto thee (Job 22:21).
>
> Commit thy way unto the Lord; trust also in him; and he shall bring it to pass (Psalm 37:5).
>
> Be of good courage, and he shall strengthen your heart, all ye that hope in the Lord. (Psalm 31:24)

The prison experiences are times to pray. Longfellow wrote, "Let one unceasing earnest prayer be, too, for light—for strength to bear our portion of the weight of care, that crushes into dumb despair one half the human race." [1] Hurtful experiences of life are not to cast you into despair, but they should cause your heart and soul to pray fervently to the Lord.

When Paul and Silas were thrown into prison, the first thing they did was pray. "And at midnight Paul and Silas prayed" (Acts 16:25). They had learned to watch unto prayer. Praying and acquainting one's self with God is what gives a person the fortitude to be able to wait, trust, commit and hold on. If allowed to do so, an imprisonment could be just the thing to elevate you to a higher plane in God.

Prison experiences are not to make you bitter, but they are a time of drawing nearer to the Lord. An unknown author of the early 1900's wrote the following about *The Philosophy Of Prayer:*

> Prayer is the most precious experience and opportunity of life.
>
> Most people do not understand its meaning and purpose.

It is not a means to get something we may desire for our convenience. It is not the act of a suppliant beggar.

It is an active, beautiful, mutual friendship between God and His children.

God is our Father. He is supremely great and wonderfully interesting.

He is the Supreme Master of affairs in the universe.

The promise—if ye abide in me—This is Unbroken Fellowship.

Prayer alone builds this.

If My words abide in you.

This is perfect obedience. Doing heroically, no matter how seemingly heavy the cross, every known duty. The Divine empowering assures strength. "Lo, I am with you." "Ye shall receive power." Divine guidance never fails.

Having passed through these precious chambers of the Divine approach—one word unlocks all the wealth of God. It is the Precious name—Jesus.

"Whatsoever ye shall ask of the Father in my name, He will give it you."

Fellowship with Jesus; Unfailing loyalty to Jesus; Perfect obedience to Jesus, gives you the right to use the name of Jesus.

It indicated you care; that you are interested in the success of Jesus' mission to the lost. It indicated to the Father that Jesus may reproduce His life through your life. So when you come in unbroken fellowship and unswerving loyalty to Jesus, that Precious name upon your lips opens the Father's measureless storehouse of blessings for others.

What supreme opportunity! [2]

THE BLESSING OF THE PRISON

Men and women through the ages have realized the power of prayer. Alfred Tennyson, the poet, wrote:

> Pray for my soul. More things are wrought by prayer
> Than the world dreams of. Wherefore let thy voice
> Rise like a fountain for me night and day.
> For what are men better than sheep or goats
> That nourish a blind life within the brain,
> If, knowing God, they lift not hands of prayer
> Both for themselves and those who call them friends?
> For so the whole round earth is every way
> Bound by gold chains about the feet of God. [3]

When you pray, things sometimes for awhile seem to get worse, but keep praying and believing—God is working something out for your good.

"In the early spring of 1877, Minnesota farmers surveyed their lands, dreading the first hordes of locusts that had caused such widespread destruction the summer before. Another such plague threatened to destroy Minnesota's rich wheatlands, spelling ruin for thousands of families.

"Suddenly Governor John S. Pillsbury proclaimed April 26 a day of fasting and prayer, urging that every man, woman and child ask divine help. A strange hush fell over the land as Minnesotans solemnly assembled to pray. Next morning the sun rose in cloudless skies. Temperatures soared to mid-summer heat. The people looked up at the skies in wonder, and to their horror, the warm earth began to stir with the dreaded insects.

"This was a strange answer! Three days passed. The unseasonable heat hatched out a vast army of locusts that threatened to engulf the entire Northwest! Then, on the fourth day the sun went down in a cold sky and that night frost gripped the earth. Most of the locusts were destroyed as surely as if fire had swept them away! When summer came the wheat waved tall and green. April 26 went down in history as the day on which a people's prayer had been answered." [4]

The prison experience is no time to quit praying; it is the time to pray like you have never prayed before. Pray until! Prayer is touching divinity! It is man taking hold of the promises of God and being able to walk boldly into the throne room of heaven and speaking directly to the Lord Jesus as commanded in Hebrews 4:16: "Let us therefore come boldly unto the throne of grace, that we may obtain mercy, and find grace to help in time of need."

It is the difficulties of life that make a person give forth words of beauty and experience that lift another soul to higher heights. A person on his knees produces the most beautiful sound.

"A maker of violins searched all his life for wood that would serve for making violins with a certain beautiful and haunting resonance. At last he succeeded when he came into possession of wood gathered from the timberline, the last stand of the trees of the Rockies, 12,000 feet above sea level. Up there where the winds blow so fiercely and steadily that the bark to windward has no chance to grow, where the branches all point one way, and where a tree to live must stay on its knees all through its life, that is where the world's most resonant wood for violins is born and lives and dies." [5]

THE BLESSING OF THE PRISON

"Strength is born in the deep silence of longsuffering hearts, not amid joy."

—Felicia Hemans

THE BLESSING OF THE PRISON

9

LIGHT IN THE PRISON

If you were allowed to choose only one thing to take to prison with you, what would it be? "The editor of a well-known London newspaper sent a letter of inquiry to one hundred important peers, members of Parliament, university professors, authors, merchants—a varied list. The inquiry was: 'Suppose you were sent to prison for three years and you could only take three books with you. Which three would you choose? Please state them in order of their importance.'

"Out of the replies, 98 put one book first on their list: the Bible...They knew that no other book could give them cheer and comfort to help in dark, difficult days." [1]

If you have the Word you have everything that is needed. It stands alone! It will shine a light into the dark circumstance and help your soul soar even though things around you look bleak.

THE BLESSING OF THE PRISON

Psalm 119:105 says, "Thy word is a lamp unto my feet, and a light unto my path."

The Word is referred to as being a fire. Fire is light. "Is not my word like as a fire? saith the Lord: and like a hammer that breaketh the rock in pieces?" (Jeremiah 23:29).

Jeremiah was cast into prison several times in his lifetime because the king did not like what he prophesied, but over and over the scripture says, *"The word of the Lord came unto Jeremiah."* Jeremiah 33:1 says, "Moreover the word of the Lord came unto Jeremiah the second time, while he was yet shut up in the court of the prison." It was the word that brought light and hope to his soul. He was not alone in a situation without hope, but he continually was honored by God and allowed to hear a word from Him.

At one particular time, in Jeremiah 36, the Lord told Jeremiah to get a roll and have a scribe write the words in ink.

> And Jeremiah commanded Baruch, saying, I am shut up; I cannot go into the house of the Lord: Therefore go thou, and read in the roll, which thou hast written from my mouth, the words of the Lord in the ears of the people in the Lord's house upon the fasting day: and also thou shalt read them in the ears of all Judah...It may be they will present their supplication before the Lord, and will return everyone from their evil way: for great is the anger and the fury that the Lord hath pronounced against the people (verses 5-7).

When Michaiah, one of the king's staff-members, heard the words he went to the king's house and delivered to all the scribes and princes all that he had heard. They then sent for

Baruch to come and read it to them. After he finished reading they told him that the king must hear it. But someone told Baruch, "Go hide thee, thou and Jeremiah; and let no man know where ye be" (verse 19).

The king sent Jehudi to fetch the roll and also appointed him to read it. After Jehudi had read three or four leaves, he cut it with a penknife, and cast it into the fire that was on the hearth. The king commanded that Baruch and Jeremiah be taken, "but the Lord hid them" (verse 26).

The word of the Lord came to Jeremiah again and said, "Take thee again another roll, and write in it all the former words that were in the first roll" (verse 28). The king tried to destroy the light of the Word by burning it by fire, but the natural fire could not destroy the fire of God's Word, because the Word of the Lord is forever settled in heaven! No amount of fiery trials can take away the power of the Word. "For the word of God is quick, and powerful, and sharper than any twoedged sword, piercing even to the dividing asunder of soul and spirit, and of the joints and marrow, and is a discerner of the thoughts and intents of the heart" (Hebrews 4:12). Nobody can read your thoughts, but God and His Word can literally go into your thought kingdom and bring light to disturbed thoughts.

"For thou wilt light my candle: the Lord my God will enlighten my darkness" (Psalm 18:28). How does He do this? The Word is a light! Psalm 119:130 says, "The entrance of thy words giveth light."

In Matthew 4, when Jesus was tempted of the devil, He used the Word of God to dispel the dark temptation. When the devil asked Him to turn the stones into bread, Jesus quoted from Deuteronomy 8:3, "Man doth not live by bread only, but by every word that proceedeth out of the mouth of the Lord doth man live." In every temptation that the devil put before Jesus, He simply said, "It is written." The light of the Word was sufficient!

As powerful as the Word was against the devil in the time of temptation, just as powerful is the Word during those times when you are walking through trouble and anguish. The psalmist wrote, "Trouble and anguish have taken hold on me: yet thy commandments are my delights" (Psalm 119:143).

Notice the word *delight* contains the word *light*. The light of the Word brings delight to the soul, although things on the outward may look devastating. There is nothing more uplifting than the Word of God when life puts you in the pit or the prison. The psalmist wrote, "My soul melteth for heaviness: strengthen thou me according to thy word" (Psalm 119:28). The Word makes the load seem lighter and dispels the gloom of the night.

The Word is a quickener! It brings life when there is no hope. The psalm says, "Remember the word unto thy servant, upon which thou hast caused me to hope. This is my comfort in my affliction: for thy word hath quickened me" (Psalm 119:49-50). *Quickened* means "to revive or make alive; to excite or stimulate."

When everything is black, it is time to get out the Word of the Lord. When all hope is gone, get out the quickener. The Word has been burned, laughed out, rejected and scorned— even legislatures have tried to keep it out of public places—but nothing can stop the power of the Word, for the Word is backed by God's power. There is no power bigger than God! It is like a cat trying to step on an elephant. It is totally impossible. Nobody can do away with the Word! It is alive forevermore.

Isaiah 40:8 says, "The grass withereth, the flower fadeth: but the word of our God shall stand for ever."

THE BLESSING OF THE PRISON

"When we are flat on our backs there is no way to look but up."

—Roger W. Babson

THE BLESSING OF THE PRISON

10

PRAISE IN THE PRISON

*P*raise is like eagle's wings. It causes one to soar in his spirit. You can be encased in plaster and still make contact with divinity, which always is an uplifter of the mind and spirit.

When some people get in trouble, they immediately start talking about it. They talk to anyone who will listen; they talk about the injustice instead of thanking God. They reason in their mind that they have a just cause to spread dirt or speak loudly about their innocence and the other person's wrong. They are looking at their situation through carnal eyes. There were several people in the Bible who did differently, and they all were visited by God or His angel.

When Daniel was plotted against and men sought his hurt, the time came when he found out about it. Watch Daniel in one of the deepest hurts of his life. He prospered in the king's court

THE BLESSING OF THE PRISON

and was elevated because of his excellent spirit, and this became too much of a bur in the hearts of those he was elevated over.

Behind his back they devised their evil plan and succeeded in getting the king's signature attached to it. When Daniel heard about the writing of the decree, which forbid anyone to ask a petition of anyone but the king for a period of thirty days, he did not go to anyone and belly-ache about the injustice done to him.

He did just the opposite. Instead of talking to man, he talked to God. Not only talked, but gave thanks, which was his regular way of praying. He had learned the power of praise and thanksgiving. "Now when Daniel knew that the writing was signed, he went into his house; and his windows being open in his chamber toward Jerusalem, he kneeled upon his knees three times a day, and gave thanks before his God, as he did aforetime" (Daniel 6:10).

It was Daniel's lifestyle to give thanksgiving to God no matter what the circumstances of his life were. This is a secret that needs to be learned early in a Christian's walk: to praise God no matter what happens!

Is this biblical? Yes! Ephesians 5:20 says, "Giving thanks **always** for **all** things unto God, and the Father in the name of our Lord Jesus Christ."

I Thessalonians 5:18 further states, "In everything give thanks, for this is the will of God in Christ Jesus concerning you."

It is the will of God for you to give praise and thanks in extenuating and troublesome times. This is what Daniel did and God sent an angel to shut the lions' mouths. Daniel was preserved because the Lord had greater things for him to do, and his attitude was one of thanksgiving instead of bitterness toward his accusers.

Attitude always determines the destiny of an individual.

What are you seeing? Do you see the rats in your prison? Do the conniving antics of those around you corrode your spirit with bitterness, or can you lift your heart and thank God even when life seems unfair? When you see only the mud and dirt of your circumstances and the littleness of your fellowman, then you have dim eyesight and small vision. People are bigger to you than God is. God has diminished and circumstances have been magnified.

The Scripture tells us to magnify the Lord, not magnify the hurt or the dirt! What is it you are magnifying? Whatever you talk about the most is what you are magnifying. Psalm 34:3 says, "O magnify the Lord with me, and let us exalt his name together." Preceding verse 3, verses 1-2 say, "I will bless the Lord at **all** times: **his praise** shall continually be in my **mouth**. My soul shall make her boast in the Lord: the humble shall hear thereof and be glad."

In Psalm 40, David is talking to the Lord and describing those that are against him. He says, "Let them be ashamed and confounded together that seek after my soul to destroy it; let them be driven backward and put to shame that wish me evil. Let them be desolate for a reward of their shame that say unto me, Aha, aha" (Psalm 40:14-15).

Notice instead of *talking about his enemies* to his friends, he is *talking to God.* He continues with the right attitude. "Let all those that seek thee rejoice and be glad in thee: let such as love thy salvation say continually, The Lord be magnified" (Psalm 40:16).

THE BLESSING OF THE PRISON

Then he remembers his hurt and asks the Lord to hurry and help him. "But I am poor and needy; yet the Lord thinketh upon me: thou art my help and my deliverer; make no tarrying, O my God" (Psalm 40:17).

Learning to praise in the prison is one of life's greatest lessons. It is Biblical and it is powerful; it brings great results. The familiar story often told about Paul and Silas must be brought to attention here. The fact is that most people with bleeding backs would not *feel* like praising the Lord.

"And when they had laid *many* stripes upon them, they cast them into prison, charging the jailor to keep them safely: who, having received such a charge, thrust them into the inner prison, and made their feet fast in the stocks" (Acts 16:23-24). When a person receives many stripes, there is much bleeding and intense pain. They proved that it does not matter where life lands you or where your feet take you; if you let the Lord be uppermost in your thoughts, He will bring you out.

"And at midnight Paul and Silas prayed, and sang praises unto God: and the prisoners heard them" (Acts 16:25). Not only did the prisoners hear them, but God heard them! "And suddenly there was a great earthquake, so that the foundations of the prison were shaken: and immediately all the doors were opened, and everyone's bands were loosed" (Acts 16:26).

It does not matter if you are in the inner or outer prison. It does not matter if your back is bleeding and your feet are in stocks. The thing that matters most is that you praise the Lord in the midnights of your life. When it is the most dark, that is the time to praise Him the most!

He inhabits the praises of His people! Praise Him whether you feel like it or not, for He is worthy! Do not praise awhile, then grumble awhile, then gossip about your problem to everyone. Continue to praise the Lord until the foundation of your prison is shaken. You shake it by praise.

"Let all those that seek thee rejoice and be glad in thee: and let such as love thy salvation say continually, Let God be magnified" (Psalm 70:4). Magnify God in the prison or during a sickness, crisis, or tragedy. Say with Job, "Blessed be the name of the Lord" (Job 1:21), even when it looks like you have lost it all.

Many things that we regard as misfortunes are blessings. Trials and crosses are often the greatest blessings in disguise, for it is only through such disciplinary processes that the character is perfected.

THE BLESSING OF THE PRISON

"The deeper the trial, the richer the gold."

—Joy Haney

THE BLESSING OF THE PRISON

11

PROSPER IN THE PRISON

Genesis 39:23 says, "The keeper of the prison looked not to anything that was under his hand; because the Lord was with him [Joseph], and that which he did, the Lord made it to prosper."

It is easier to just give up and succumb to despair and hopelessness when you encounter a prison experience. And although true Christians may struggle with these emotions, they do not let them have victory over them. They turn the negative experience into a positive opportunity. When Martin Luther was imprisoned in Wartburg Castle, he translated the Bible into a language for many people to read. When John Bunyan was imprisoned in Bedford, he wrote one of the most popular books ever.

"John Bunyan, by trade a tinker and by nature headstrong and passionate, lived a carefree and reckless life—until he

THE BLESSING OF THE PRISON

became a Christian. Then he turned his immense energies into publicly preaching the gospel that had redeemed him—until he was thrown into jail. (It was contrary to English law for dissenters from the State religion to hold public meetings.) Even in the face of imprisonment the freedom-loving nature did not despair. During the twelve years of confinement in Bedford jail, Bunyan supported his family by making shoe laces, and affirmed his Christian faith by writing *Pilgrim's Progress*. His book became the most popular and effective tract in propagating Christianity ever written." [1]

When a person is cast into a literal prison or a prison formed by circumstances or people, he has the opportunity to bless others. He can preach the gospel to those that need it, thinking of others instead of self. He can write letters of encouragement that will bring a rejoicing to many hearts, such as Paul did. He may learn true forgiveness such as Corrie ten Boom did towards the guards who were like beasts at Ravensbruck Prison during World War II. An unknown author wrote:

Teach me to live! 'Tis far easier to die—
Gently and silently to pass away—
On earth's long night to close the heavy eye,
And awaken in the realms of glorious day.

Teach me that harder lesson—how to live.
To serve Thee in the darkest path of life:
Arm me for conflict—fresh vigor give,
And make me more than conqueror in the strife.

Teach me to live! Thy purpose to fulfill;
Bright for Thy glory let my taper shine;

Each day renew, remold this stubborn will;
Closer round Thee my heart's affection twine.

Teach me to live! For self and sin no more.
But use the time remaining to me yet,
Not mine own pleasure seeking, as before—
Wasting no precious hours in vain regret.

Teach me to live! No idler let me be,
But in Thy service hand and heart employ,
Prepared to do Thy bidding cheerfully—
Be this my highest and holiest joy.

Teach me to live! My daily cross to bear;
No murmur though I bend beneath its load.
Only be with me. Let me feel Thee near:
Thy smile sheds gladness on the darkest road.

Teach me to live! And find my life in Thee—
Looking from earth and earthly things away;
Let me not falter, but untiringly press on;
And gain new strength and power each day. [2]

You can choose either to live or die. You will curse your surroundings and wish for better things, or you will just *prosper or grow* where you are placed or planted. There are some things that cannot be born in perfect situations. It is the rugged atmosphere that sometimes produces the greatest things. E.E. Edgar shares the following story.

THE BLESSING OF THE PRISON

Sir Alexander Fleming made his discovery of penicillin while working in a dusty old laboratory. A mold spore, blown in through a window, landed on a culture plate he was about to examine.

Some years later, he was taken on a tour of an up-to-date research lab, a gleaming, air-conditioned, dust-free, super-sterile setting. "What a pity you did not have a place like this to work in," his guide said. "What you could have discovered in such surroundings!"

"Not penicillin," Fleming observed dryly. [3]

The best things many times are born out of less-than-desired circumstances, adversity and often pain. Look not at the ramshackle, falling-apart situation, but look at the possibilities that are available through it. Do not be like Henry J. Ellsworth, commissioner of the U.S. Patent office. He assured people that his resignation was really of no great concern. "'Mankind,' he declared, 'has already achieved all of which it is capable. There will be not more inventions requiring patents.'

"The year was 1844—before the steamboat, the telegraph cable under the ocean, the electric light, the telephone, and a host of other inventions that came along during the next half century." [4]

Do not close your mind just because circumstances or people have tried to put bars around you. Nothing can shut you up but yourself (and God, of course). No demon, no lie, no pain, nothing can take away your hope and power to prosper, even in the prison. Remember these scriptures when you are placed in a prison not of your own making:

...Greater is he that is in you than he that is in the world (I John 4:4).

...If God be for us, who can be against us? (Romans 8:31).

I can do all things through Christ which strengtheneth me (Philippians 4:13).

...God is faithful, who will not suffer you to be tempted above that ye are able... (I Corinthians 10:13).

No weapon that is formed against thee shall prosper... (Isaiah 54:17).

...Yet have I not seen the righteous forsaken, nor his seed begging bread (Psalm 37:25).

You can prosper even in the prison as Joseph and many others did. It is there that you will probably do your greatest work. Men and women down through the ages have gone to prison for ideas which benefited mankind in a temporal way. Charles Goodyear was repeatedly imprisoned for debt while developing his inventions, and perfected one while he was in jail. He could not convince anyone outside of his family of the value of his discovery, but his perseverance in and out of the prison finally brought to the world vulcanized rubber.

Your imprisonment may not be because of a dream such as Charles Goodyear's, but it could be a dream or vision involving furthering the kingdom of God on the earth. The time of emotional pain, rejection, suffering, and false accusation which accompanied Joseph in his time of imprisonment was not brought on by what he did, but by what he dreamed. God had a plan for greater things in his life, and part of the plan involved the mistreatment by his brethren and those he loved and respected. Although he suffered mistreatment, he still prospered even in the prison.

"Affliction comes to us, not to make us sad but sober; not to make us sorry but wise."

—Henry Ward Beecher

THE BLESSING OF THE PRISON

12

WAIT PATIENTLY IN THE PRISON

The most difficult thing to do is wait! But it is the waiting that produces the fruit. It is the waiting that produces the gold and silver as the refiner watches what is taking place inside the fire. There is the waiting period for the flowers to grow to show beauty, the seed of corn to grow to produce food, and the young trees to grow to be able to give shade. One season waits for another. All of life is involved with waiting.

Psalm 27:14 says it well, "Wait on the Lord: be of good courage, and he shall strengthen thine heart: wait, I say, on the Lord." In this one verse, we are told twice to wait on the Lord. *Wait* means "to look unto the Lord with expectancy." While you are waiting He will give you strength. Waiting with courage is the ideal. Courage faces difficulties with bravery, determina-

THE BLESSING OF THE PRISON

tion and dignity. It stands firm while adversity tries to sweep you down into a pit of cold despair.

There is a stillness that accompanies waiting. Psalm 46:10 says, "Be still, and know that I am God." There are some things that you cannot do, but God can. There are times to cease from your worrisome activity, and to be still and let God do that which is impossible for you to do.

Two anonymous authors wrote the following poems that say it well:

> If we bravely resolve to do our part,
> And bear our griefs with a patient heart
> And free from all repining,
>
> We shall be held to a higher way,
> To a better work than we do today,
> And find love's sunlight shining;
>
> For truth of spirit and strength of soul
> Will make the darkest cloud unroll,
> And show its silver lining. [1]

LEARN TO WAIT

> Learn to wait—life's hardest lesson,
> Learned, perchance, through blinding tears
> While the heart-throbs, sadly march
> To the tread of passing years.
>
> Learn to wait—Hope's slow fruition;

Faint not, though the way seem long;
There is joy in each condition—
Hearts, though suffering, may grow strong.

Constant sunshine, however welcome,
Ne'er would ripen fruit or flower;
Giant oaks owe half their greatness
To the scathing tempest's power.

Thus a soul, untouched by sorrow,
Aims not at a higher state;
Joy seeks not a brighter morrow:
Only sad hearts learn to wait.

Human strength and human greatness
Spring not from life's sunny side;
Heroes must be more than driftwood
Floating on a waveless tide. [2]

    The opposite of waiting on the Lord is anxiety, fretfulness, and worry. Worry causes the worrier to be drained of his strength. Author Ian Maclaren wrote, "What does your anxiety do? It does not empty tomorrow, brother, of its sorrow; but ah! it empties today of its strength. It does not make you escape the evil; it makes you unfit to cope with it if it comes." [3]

    Waiting expectantly, watching with prayer, working towards, and enduring through is the way to win! There are no mistakes with God. The Bible says, "The steps of a good man are ordered by the Lord..." (Psalm 37:23). Since this is so, and since God knows where you are at all times, why worry and fret? He has only good things in store for you. So what if there

THE BLESSING OF THE PRISON

are times when you are bruised and bleeding and the bumps of life jolt you off your comfortable seat? So what if your progress is barred and the shocks of life test your courage bold? It has not been promised to you that the road would be smooth and all would be well.

There are times when the plow of life plows deep and the steel blades break up the fallow ground of the heart. The heart feels the sharp pain and staggers beneath the load, but wait on the Lord, He is working something out for your good.

Mrs. Charles E. Cowman wrote,

> God does not use the plough and harrow without intention! Where God ploughs He intends to sow! His ploughing is proof He is for, and not against us! The husbandman is never so near the land as when he is ploughing it: the very time when we are tempted to think that He hath forsaken us!
>
> The ploughman is a proof that he thinks you of value and worth cultivating—and He does not waste His ploughing on the barren sand. He will not plough continually, but only for a time, and for a definite purpose. Soon He will close that process. "Doth the ploughman plough continually to sow! Doth he continually open and break up the clods of his ground?" (Isaiah 28:24, RV). Verily no! Soon, aye soon, we shall through these painful processes, and by His gentle showers of grace, become His fruitful land. "The desolate land shall be tilled...and they shall say, This land that was desolate is become like the garden of Eden" (Ezekiel 36:34,35). And thus shall we be a praise unto Him.
>
> "Someone must go through sore travail of soul before a life movement, outwardly visible, can be born," said

Josephine Butler. The one who seeks release from the process of fruitage would expel the furrows from the face of Lincoln, and make Paul a mere esthetic—would rob the Divine Sufferer of His sanctity. We cannot have the result of the harvest without the process! The price must be paid. [4]

The waiting many times is to stave off disaster. James H. McConkey wrote in his tract *Believing is Seeing* the following:

> You have been taking a long and wearisome railroad journey. For hours you have been traveling through the dust and heat. You are nearing home, and brook with impatience each delay. At midnight you are awakened by the slowing of your train. It bumps, jars and creaks, and finally comes to a standstill. You wait, and wait. You peer out into the gloom with your face pressed against the car window. Five, ten, twenty minutes pass. Still all is quiet, with no sign of a move. You drum at the window pane. You turn wearily in your berth. You wonder when the weary wait will end. Presently there is a sound in the distance. The rattle and clatter come nearer. Then there is a rush, a roar, the red glare of a great fiery eye and the monster engine and its trail of coaches sweeps by you in an instant and is swallowed up in the encircling darkness. You have waited long. Now you can see. You see in vision the awful death which would have come to you had you gone on. You see the wise forethought which kept you waiting on that track. It was a passing siding and the one safe thing to do was to wait. Had you gone on it would have been to the wreckage and death of a collision.

Is your heart there and your body here? Are you eager for service and yet hindered on every side? Is the horizon of life so narrowed by circumstances as to become almost unbearable? Yet God's waiting time is best for you. Wait—and you will see barriers razed. Wait—and you will see circumstances change. Wait—and you will see God bringing things to pass beyond all your dreams. Wait and you shall see. For "He worketh for him that waits for Him." [5]

"Affliction, like the iron-smith, shapes as it smites."

—Christian Nestell Bovee

THE BLESSING OF THE PRISON

13

THE BEST IS YET TO COME

"A beautiful, very beautiful stained-glass window in a cathedral was the object of attraction to many tourists. One night an awful storm raged; the whole window frame blew in, and the glass smashed in atoms on the floor. The sorrowful people of the city gathered up the fragments, placed them in a box and removed them to the crypt. One day a stranger came, and asked permission to see them and if he might take them away. 'Yes,' they said, 'we have no use for them.' Later came a mysterious invitation to some of those city authorities from a well-known artist in stained glass. A curtain was removed in his studio, and there was their beautiful window, only more, much more beautiful than before—a gift from the artist to take home." [1]

This was written by a man who had suffered a nervous breakdown from much pressure and affliction of mind. He

THE BLESSING OF THE PRISON

found out that there is always a better day when the Lord enters the picture. You can either grow disillusioned with life and its experiences, or you can look ahead to life with expectancy—this life and the life hereafter.

This is what Elizabeth Redfield chose to do. She knew the joy and pain of raising a family, but did not let any of her experiences make her old and bitter. Seventy-five years ago she wrote with exuberance the following:

> I am a fifty-six-year-old grandmother. Both my grandmothers had passed on long before that age, yet I feel that I am only on the threshold of the bigness of life.
>
> As a Civil War orphan my educational advantages were meager. When, at the age of nineteen, I married a man as poor as myself, I seemingly fortified the barrier that lay between me and the world of accomplishment.
>
> I bore four children, bringing up three of them. Painstakingly and conscientiously, I taught them morality, honor, and self-reliance. I cooked their food, ofttimes helping earn it. I washed and ironed and knit and sewed for them. At eight o'clock they were sent to bed, while I read and studied for the next two hours that I might become a more intelligent mother.
>
> After they were out of the home nest I took a business course, working my way and graduated just before my fiftieth birthday. Then I went into a newspaper office—and one of my lifelong dreams had come true.
>
> Yesterday, I spent in God's country, the open spaces and the long roads of the Big Southwest. Today I am in the man-made cities of the East. I have had six months'

instructions in art in one of your wonderful public night schools; have visited art galleries and studios.

I haven't adjectives to tell you what I think of your public libraries, but they are manna to my starved intellect.

I attend lectures galore. My body sits entranced before the great opera and concert singers, while my soul soars to Heaven with their melody. Only last night I laughed, cried and sang with Sir Harry Lauder.

Time is the only limit and lack of funds the only restriction. I have sat in a man-made battleship on a God-made ocean—oh, the wonderful, wonderful things I have experienced! All, all, dreams come true.

Tomorrow I shall add the past to the present and write, write, write.

Ah, dear God! The best is yet to be, the last of life, for which the first was made. [2]

Joseph, of whom this book was inspired, had this same spirit. He did not let yesterday's hurts become his grave. He realized that God was faithful even in the bad times. The best was yet to be for him, for because of the prison experience, Joseph met the man that eventually led him to the throne. His dream was fulfilled and many people were saved. "But as for you, ye thought evil against me; but God meant it unto good, to bring to pass, as it is this day, to *save much* people alive" (Genesis 50:20).

The same transpired in the life of Daniel. Because of Daniel's dreadful trip to the lions' den, many people were made aware of his God. The king had gone very early to the den and inquired how Daniel was doing. When he found out that the angel of the Lord had protected him, the king gave the order to

THE BLESSING OF THE PRISON

have Daniel brought out and the wicked men to be thrown in instead.

> Then King Darius wrote unto all people, nations, and languages, that dwell in all the earth; Peace be multiplied unto you. I make a decree, That in every dominion of my kingdom men tremble and fear before the God of Daniel: for he is the living God, and stedfast forever...He delivereth and rescueth, and he worketh signs and wonders in heaven and in earth, who hath delivered Daniel from the power of the lions. So this Daniel prospered... (Daniel 6:25-28).

An unknown author wrote,

> We have begun to enter into the real delight and joy of our living only when we realize that the best of life is that part that is yet to be, what we have not yet attained, what, once we have attained it, God in His goodness will make us discontented with, and set us on after the better things. [3]

Do not be dismayed or let your heart be troubled; God is working for your good according to His purpose. His ways are above our ways, but He doeth all things well! The key is to realize that the best is yet to come, and to not grumble, but to trust in God and give Him praise for whatever is happening in your life.

You may wonder why God allowed it. You are not alone. Jeremiah, the prophet, asked basically the same question. "Moreover Jeremiah said unto king Zedekiah, What have I offended against thee, or against thy servants, or against this people, that ye have put me in prison?" (Jeremiah 37:18). He did not understand it, and you may not understand it either.

Jeremiah thought he had it bad, but things got worse for him. He went from prison to the dungeon. "And they let down Jeremiah with cords. And in the dungeon there was no water, but mire: so Jeremiah sunk in the mire" (Jeremiah 38:16). Things often get worse before they get better, as they did for Jeremiah. He sank lower and lower, but eventually he was released.

God has an appointed time for you to come out of your prison. Psalm 146:7 contains the most beautiful words in the world to a prisoner: "...The Lord looseth the prisoners." You will emerge from the prison a better person. One of the reasons Christ came was to be able to enter into a situation that life brings and "to bring out the prisoners from the prison" (Isaiah 42:7). Life is not perfect. Hurtful things will transpire, but the Lord will bring you through victoriously!

Hope in the prison. Never give up that golden thread of expectancy. It may be only a thread, but that is all you need to see you through. The poet William Pierson Merrill wrote:

Expect the best! It lies not in the past,
God even keeps the good wine till the last.
Beyond are nobler work and sweeter rest.
Expect the best. [4]

Things will get better. Life is a time of preparation for the future. This is not the final act; it is only a stage rehearsal for the finer, more wonderful aspect of eternity, which is forever! God always has something good in store for you, so expect the

THE BLESSING OF THE PRISON

best in God as He orders your steps. George H. Hepworth wrote,

> Amid the drudgery and hardship of life keep that truth in mind and it will clear the fogs away and leave you in sunshine. We are on the road home, and the way is sometimes dark and dreary, but when we get there we shall see that every experience of earth was intended to fit us for the higher joys of heaven. [5]

NOTES

Chapter 2

1. Tan, Paul Lee, ThD. *Encyclopedia of 7,700 Illustrations: Signs of the Times*, (Rockville, Maryland: Assurance Publishers, 1979), #6861
2. Dean C. Dutton, Ph.D., arr. & comp., *Quests and Conquests*, (Guthrie, OK: Live Service Publishing Co., 1923), #28
3. Ibid #86
4. Mrs. Charles E. Cowman, *Streams in the Desert, Vol. Two*, (Grand Rapids, Michigan: Zondervan Publishing House, 1966), Excerpt taken from March 2
5. Tan, *Encyclopedia of 7,700 Illustrations*, #6852
6. Ibid., #6847
7. Dutton, *Quests and Conquests*, #1101
8. Tan, *Encyclopedia of 7,700 Illustrations*, #6878
9. Ibid., #6885
10. Dutton, *Quests and Conquests*, #79

11. Cowman, *Streams in the Desert, Vol. Two*, Writings from Beecher on February 23
12. Ibid., Quote from J.H. Evans on October 1

Chapter 3

1. Dutton, *Quests and Conquests*, #1103
2. Tan, *Encyclopedia of 7,700 Illustrations*, #6858
3. Cowman, *Streams in the Desert, Vol. Two*, Quote from A.C. Dixon on December 2
4. Ibid, Quote from George Matheson on January 18
5. Tan, *Encyclopedia of 7,700 Illustrations* #6579

Chapter 4

1. Tan, *Encyclopedia of 7,700 Illustrations*, #937
2. Ibid., #939
3. Ibid., #941
4. Ibid., #3845
5. Ibid., #3850

Chapter 5

1. Cowman, *Streams in the Desert, Vol. Two*, Quote from James McConkey on September 16
2. Ibid., Quote from Dr. Edward T. Sullivan on January 31
3. Ibid., Quote from Rev. Hugh Macmillan on November 14
4. Dutton, *Quests and Conquests*, *#531*

Notes

Chapter 6

1. Tan, *Encyclopedia of 7,700 Illustrations*, #645
2. Ibid., #6879
3. Ibid., #4965

Chapter 7

1. Dutton, *Quests and Conquests*, #980-C13
2. Ibid., #243
3. Ibid., #169
4. Ibid., #1037
5. Tan, *Encyclopedia of 7,700 Illustrations*, #3500

Chapter 8

1. Dutton, *Quests and Conquests*, #61
2. Ibid., #487
3. Ibid., #1105
4. Tan, *Encyclopedia of 7,700 Illustrations*, #2489
5. Ibid., #6906

Chapter 9

1. Tan, *Encyclopedia of 7,700 Illustrations*, #408

Chapter 11

1. Cowman, *Streams in the Desert, Vol. Two*, Excerpt from February 2
2. Dutton, *Quests and Conquests*, #494-A

3. Tan, *Encyclopedia of 7,700 Illustrations*, #4819
4. Ibid., #4805

Chapter 12

1. Dutton, *Quests and Conquests*, #111
2. Ibid., #42
3. Ibid., #46-C
4. Cowman, *Streams in the Desert, Vol. Two,* July 25
5. Ibid., Taken from James H. McConkey on November 28

Chapter 13

1. Cowman, *Streams in the Desert, Vol. Two,* Writings from James McConkey on June 6
2. Dutton, *Quests and Conquests*, #88
3. Ibid., #33
4. Lillian Eichler Watson, ed. & comm., *Light from Many Lamps,* (New York, NY: Simon & Schuster, 1951), p. 276
5. Dutton, *Quests and Conquests*, #139